Developing
Observation Skills

Carolyn S. Swallow

MCGRAW-HILL SERIES IN SPECIAL EDUCATION

Robert M. Smith, Consulting Editor

Cartwright and Cartwright   *Developing Observation Skills*
Smith   *Clinical Teaching: Methods of Instruction for the Retarded*
Smith   *Introduction to Mental Retardation*
Worell and Nelson   *Managing Instruction Problems:*
A Case Study Workbook

Developing Observation Skills

Carol A. Cartwright
G. Phillip Cartwright

Associate Professors of Education
College of Education, The Pennsylvania State University

McGraw-Hill Book Company

New York   St. Louis   San Francisco   Düsseldorf   Johannesburg
Kuala Lumpur   London   Mexico   Montreal   New Delhi   Panama
Paris   São Paulo   Singapore   Sydney   Tokyo   Toronto

Developing Observation Skills

1234567890 DODO 7987654

Library of Congress Cataloging in Publication Data

Cartwright, Carol A   date
    Developing observation skills.

    (McGraw-Hill series in special education)
    1.   Educational tests and measurements. 2.   Observation (Psychology) 3.   Teachers, Training of.
I.   Cartwright, Glen Phillip, 1937-   joint author.
II.   Title.
LB3051.C37   371.3   73-14935
ISBN 0-07-010184-1

This book was set in Press Roman by Creative Book Services, division of McGregor & Werner, Inc. The editor was Robert C. Morgan; the designer was Creative Book Services; and the production supervisor was Paula Sturim.
R. R. Donnelley & Sons Company was the printer and binder.

iv

To Catherine and Stephen

Contents

Preface

Developing Observation Skills is about observation and the role it plays in instructional decision making. We view the teacher as a seeker of data and as an instructional decision maker. Teachers need to use evidence as a basis for instructional decisions and some of this evidence needs to be obtained through observation.

Chapter One addresses the question: Is observation necessary? The response is an emphatic "Yes," with most of the chapter devoted to convincing the reader of the need to use observation. Subsequent chapters are presentations of the methods of designing and using observation procedures. Chapter Two identifies the general principles, procedures, and problems applicable to all observation situations. Chapters Three, Four, and Five deal with specific types of records used for observation: behavior tallying and charting, checklists, rating scales and participation charts, and anecdotal records.

The orientation of the book is practical. There are no references to theory and no research reports. We've written the book in what we think is a concise, readable way, and we've provided numerous examples and illustrations to elaborate on the essentials of observation presented in the book. The examples encompass levels from preschool through late elementary and secondary school. A wide variety of content areas are represented in the examples. In addition, examples involving specialists in areas such as reading, speech, and special education are given. Activities designed to extend skills are provided for each chapter.

Given the scope and variety of examples and activities, we expect teachers in all areas and levels will find the book helpful. *Developing Observation Skills* will fit into such teacher preparation courses as Introduction to Education, Methods of Education, Practicum in Education, Early Childhood Education Methods, and Introduction to Special Education.

It is always difficult to be sure that all those deserving of thanks actually get recognized when a project such as this is undertaken. Being a wife-husband team on this project means that we have relied on some support systems to keep the family going while we worked on the book. And so, we extend warm thank-yous to those who kept our home and family operating smoothly. We also acknowledge the help of our typing team of Diane Bloom, Jan Carroll, and Karen Lewis. We extend special thanks to Jim Campbell for preparing the illustrations. Finally, we want to express our appreciation to our colleagues who have reviewed the manuscript in its various stages and offered many helpful suggestions.

Carol A. Cartwright
G. Phillip Cartwright

ONE

Necessity of observation

You have probably watched enough television to know that the usual image presented for lawyers and doctors is that they function as detectives. Lawyers are pictured as gathering clues, uncovering eye witnesses, solving cases, and saving their clients from dire fate. Doctors relentlessly track down new treatments and thwart the spread of disease.

Doctors and lawyers seek data. Lawyers know that hunches won't stand up in court, and that they have a better chance of convincing the jury in favor of their client if they have a large amount of factual information to present. Similarly, a doctor knows he can't indiscriminately prescribe medication, perform surgery, and initiate other treatment procedures; he needs diagnostic data—facts about the patient's symptoms, medical history, results of tests—in order to make decisions and enlist the patient's cooperation and permission. In general, we would say that both doctors and lawyers operate as decision makers and use factual information, whenever possible, as the basis for the medical and legal decisions they are expected to make.

Although seldom described in situations as glamorous as those for the "detective" lawyer and the "detective" doctor, teachers are detectives too. Teachers should assemble as much factual information as possible before making

instructional decisions. In this chapter we'll take a careful look at both the kinds of information needed and the nature of instructional decisions teachers are expected to make.

If we were to take a close look at the various facets of the detective's job and then if we were to look closely at the roles implemented by teachers, we would find many parallels. We feel that teachers must behave as detectives in order to be effective with learners. That is, teachers must seek out diagnostic data, facts about the learners' problems, academic records, and test results so that they can make intelligent instructional decisions. Another way of adding extra force to this idea would be to say: if teachers do not function as detectives, learners will not learn. This chapter is devoted to convincing you of the reasonableness of this view of the teacher as a "seeker of data" and instructional decision maker, and informing you about the reasons underlying the use of observation as an information-gathering method.

When you complete reading this chapter and the associated activities, you should be able to:

1. Describe how you would convince a colleague of the necessity for using observation
2. Differentiate between examples of nonobservable processes and characteristics and examples of observable behaviors indicative of processes and characteristics

3. Draw reasonable inferences about the characteristics and/or processes affecting the learner when given a set of behavioral evidence about a learner
4. Decide if observation should be used as the assessment method when given descriptions of behaviors expected of learners
5. Generate an example to describe each of several instructional decision-making situations requiring observation as the assessment procedure

MAKING INSTRUCTIONAL DECISIONS

Observation is a process of systematically looking at and recording behavior for the purpose of making instructional decisions. While experts may disagree slightly about the specific instructional decisions required of the classroom teacher, there is general agreement about classes or groups of instructional decisions that must be made. These groups were derived from an analysis of the typical behaviors of classroom teachers, the aspects of the environment or situation within which teaching and learning usually occur, and from an analysis of the other people who are likely to be involved in the teaching process: the learner, the teacher, other learners, others in the school, and parents. Our listing of groups of instructional decisions is as follows:

1. Teachers must make decisions about what to teach—what most people would call deciding on the objectives.
2. Teachers must make decisions about how to sequence objectives and teaching procedures.
3. They need to decide how to teach—what many people refer to as the need to decide on the appropriate teaching methods or procedures.
4. Teachers must decide what materials to use and how to present them to learners.
5. They need to determine how to manage behavior within the classroom situation and in other situations for which they are responsible—in other words, deciding how to discipline.
6. They need to decide how to organize the time that is available during the school day.
7. Teachers must make decisions about how to group children for instruction.

8. They need to make decisions regarding how to set up the classroom environment.

9. They must decide both what to evaluate and how to evaluate the progress made by the learners toward objectives as well as the effectiveness of new instructional strategies.

10. Teachers must consider whether they need to enlist the aid of resource persons, and if they decide they do need help from resource persons (including professionals, others both within and outside of the school, and parents), they must decide whom to ask for help.

The listing of groups of instructional decisions covers in a general way just about all the elements that go together to make up the act of teaching. Thus, it can be said that observation permeates the entire teaching process by assisting the teacher in making the decisions required in effective teaching.

BEHAVIORS, CHARACTERISTICS, AND PROCESSES

It should become apparent as you proceed through this book that we emphasize the importance of observing children's *behavior*. It is almost trivial to point out that observational methods require something to observe. That "something" is behavior—anything that can be seen, heard, counted, or measured. In this section we will attempt to give you some basic information about behavior and the related ideas of characteristics and processes.

All people are constantly behaving. The number of behaviors exhibited by any one individual during a single day is staggering. And, what is most important, behaviors are out in the open—they can be observed.

But behaviors do not just magically happen. Behaviors result from something and this "something" may be many things. Suppose you are driving a car and you hear a train whistle; you know from past experience that a train whistle indicates a train is coming soon, and you react, or behave, by pressing your foot on the brake and stopping the car so you don't collide with the train. Suppose you walk into the house around dinner time; you smell something cooking and you know from past experience that the particular odor is roast beef, and you might react, or behave, by saying, "It smells like we're going to have roast beef for dinner."

A learner processes information in much the same way. He looks at a word, he knows from past experience that that particular combination of letters makes up the word *dog*, and he says, or behaves, by saying the word *dog*. Learners also exhibit many behaviors of a nonacademic nature during the time they are in school. A boy has brought a baseball to school and has left it on his desk. He notices that another boy in the class is walking near his desk, he sees the other boy pick up the baseball, and he reacts, or behaves, by saying, "Hey, that's my baseball! Put it down!"

All of these brief examples, of both in-school and out-of-school situations and academic and nonacademic situations, indicate that behaviors do not occur in and of themselves. Something happens prior to the behavior which triggers a particular response or behavior in the individual. Therefore, we can say with some degree of certainty that some behaviors are the observable products of certain characteristics of individuals or of certain processes going on within individuals. Finally, some behaviors are also the direct result of other factors or people in the child's environment.

Behavior Is the Proof of Learning

We will think of a *process* as any internal, nonobservable physiological, cognitive, or emotional activity. We have said that behaviors can be observed and that processes cannot be directly observed. We have also said that certain behaviors can be associated with certain processes.

Jimmy is a first grader. Right now he is devoting a considerable amount of time and effort in his reading program to the development of a sight vocabulary. We will think of the *development* of a sight vocabulary as a *process.* As a process, the development of a sight vocabulary is not directly observable. We cannot look at Jimmy and say, "Yes, he has a sight vocabulary," or "No, he doesn't have a sight vocabulary." If Jimmy has developed a sight vocabulary, however, he should be able to exhibit some observable behaviors which we generally think of as being associated with the process of developing a sight vocabulary. Let's take a look at a number of behaviors which Jimmy is able to exhibit and which indicate that Jimmy is developing a sight vocabulary.

Over a period of several weeks, Jimmy did the following things (he displayed these behaviors). When shown flashcards with certain vocabulary words printed on them, Jimmy *pronounced* the words correctly without hesitation. When shown flashcards with certain vocabulary words printed on them, Jimmy *selected* the cards correctly and without hesitation as the teacher pronounced each word. Given a series of pictures and a series of cards with words to accompany the pictures printed on them, Jimmy *matched* the picture cards and word cards correctly and without hesitation. Jimmy can repeat these three basic behaviors—pronouncing, selecting, and matching—over and over with fifty different sight vocabulary words.

Thus, comparing Jimmy's behavior before and after several weeks of practice with flashcards will indicate that a process (the development of sight vocabulary) has taken place.

Let's consider some observable behaviors which indicate that three-year-old Mary is gaining the processes of *generalization* and *discrimination* as she develops language competence. (Remember that generalization and discrimination cannot be directly observed; they are processes. But the behaviors associated with the processes can be observed.) Some of Mary's behaviors associated with generalization are behaviors such as: (1) when looking at pictures in a magazine, Mary correctly *labels* the chairs regardless of size, color, or style of chair pictured; and (2) whenever she is outdoors playing and she encounters a dog, she *says,* "I see a dog," regardless of size, color, or breed of the dog. Some of Mary's behaviors associated with discrimination are behaviors such as: (1) when shown pictures of a cow and a horse of similar size and coloring, Mary *labels* each picture correctly; and (2) when shown a series of pairs of pictures, Mary can *tell* if pictures in the pair are the same or different. In this instance, observing Mary's behaviors over a period of time will assist Mary's nursery school teacher in making the decision that Mary is ready for certain kinds of activities that require a certain level of ability in generalization and discrimination.

Needless to say, processes are the cornerstones of development. Development of the child from an infant to a mature adult depends on a number of internal and external processes. However, none of these are observable except as stationary slices of behavior caught at a given moment in time. A behavior is an instance of a process, its status at that particular time.

Characteristics

We will think of a *characteristic* as a predisposition to behave in a certain way under certain circumstances. We cannot directly observe the predisposition but we can observe the behaviors. Charles is a fourth grader. Over the years he has developed a pattern of behavior such that, if we were to observe him for a period of time each day for a week, we would very likely observe behaviors such as these:

1. Charles brought a baseball to school one day and, when the teacher told him to put it in his desk, he cried and said, "I can't leave it there; someone will take it."
2. Charles was sitting in the library looking at a book about machines; another boy sat down next to him and Charles clenched the book tightly and said, "Don't touch this book."

3. Another boy picked up a pencil from Charles' desk intending to use it for just a minute; Charles said, "That's mine. Put it back," stamping his foot down hard.

These and other similar behaviors would lead us to characterize Charles as a boy who is overly concerned about his possessions. He behaves inappropriately when he feels his possessions are threatened.

Thus, the concept *characteristic* is quite useful in making instructional decisions. Knowledge of a given child's characteristics, or predisposition to behave in certain ways, reduces somewhat the number of instructional strategies or materials that might logically be used in an instructional program for the child.

BEHAVIORS AND INFERENCES

But remember—only behaviors can be observed; the processes and the characteristics which caused the behaviors are out of sight. They can be *inferred,* but they cannot be observed. They are not immediately obvious to an onlooker. This is not to say that the processes and characteristics are not important; they are. It is simply to say that we have a problem when we try to identify the processes and characteristics since they are not directly observable. The events preceding, accompanying, and following the behavior can also be observed, and very often this information will be useful when we draw inferences and conclusions, and arrive at decisions about learners. We should think broadly about the preceding, accompanying, and following events and include in our collection of data such items as time, place, other people involved, objects in the environment, and behaviors displayed by others.

Remember also that a learner's behaviors can be observed. And, we have something else on our side. There is a fairly extensive background of knowledge accumulated which tells us that certain behaviors, those things which can be observed, are very often related to certain processes and characteristics, those things which cannot be directly observed. Therefore, even though we cannot see a process or a characteristic directly, we can make a reasoned judgment about whether or not it exists on the basis of the behaviors being exhibited by an individual. What we do is make an inference about the presence or absence of characteristics and processes based on behavioral evidence. By definition, this behavioral evidence is observable and others can look at it and make some decision about whether or not they agree with the inference that has been made based on the evidence.

Even though there is some information available about which behaviors are usually related to certain characteristics and processes, this body of information is by no means complete. For example, we cannot be sure of the inference we should draw when we hear a student say, "I like arithmetic." Is he making this statement, which is, of course, a behavior, because he thinks we want to hear him say that? Is he making the statement because his friend made a similar statement a few minutes ago? Is he making the statement because his parents told him that the teacher will like you if you tell her that you like arithmetic? We can never really be completely sure. Therefore, one of the critical concerns of a teacher must be to maintain constant vigilance regarding the question: What kinds of behaviors are "reasonable" for making inferences about the characteristics and processes of interest to the teacher?

Even though we can never be absolutely sure of the accuracy of the inference made, we can be more sure that the inference is justified when we base the inference on behaviors than when we do not. Many of you are acquainted with teachers who are in the habit of making statements such as, "Billy is really finally understanding addition." When asked, "How do you know?" or when requested to "prove it," these same teachers stumble and stammer and are hard pressed to give a respectable response. This is clearly a case in which the teacher has not been aware of his role as a detective in teaching. And this teacher has probably been making instructional decisions haphazardly. This pattern of behavior suggests that the teacher has made an inference which is not based on behavioral evidence. The teacher may not even be aware that it is necessary to base inference on behavioral evidence. They are likely to maintain that teachers "just automatically know" certain things. We don't agree.

Accuracy of Inferences

It is possible to increase the probable accuracy of inferences by using more than one behavior as evidence. Patterns or clusters of related, similar behaviors will emerge, and these sets of behaviors are much preferred to using a single behavior for the purpose of making inferences. The preference for using several rather than one behavior exists because one piece of evidence could easily be canceled out by some other pieces of evidence, and if we make an inference on that one piece of evidence, we may not know what other cancellation effects there are. The moral for the teacher here is that the more behavioral evidence—both about the learner and about the other events—he is able to collect, the more sure he can be that the inference he draws from that evidence is reasonable and justified.

A Pause for Some Examples

Let's consider two different situations. In the first, the teacher makes an inference about a child on the basis of two pieces of behavioral evidence. In the second situation, the teacher collects many more clues—observes more behaviors—before making an inference about the child.

Here's the first situation. Mary exhibited these two behaviors: (1) after several trials, Mary *repeated* the definition of a set; and (2) when the teacher showed Mary a set of five spoons and asked Mary what word should be used to fill in the blank in the sentence, "Here is a _____ of five spoons," Mary *said*, "Set." On the basis of these two behaviors, the teacher concluded that Mary had an understanding of the concept of a *set*. Those of you who are familiar with the concept of set and who are also aware of the difference between rote memory and understanding, will quickly see that the teacher may well be wrong in concluding that Mary understands the concept of set. So far, all we really know is that Mary has memorized a definition and a label about sets.

Here's the second situation. Let's suppose that, in addition to the two behaviors described in the first situation, the teacher also observed Mary displaying behaviors such as these: (1) when given a box of play dishes and eating utensils and directions to make a set of cups, Mary *selects* the cups from the box and *groups* them together to make a set of cups; (2) when the teacher makes a set of forks and a set of spoons and a set of knives and gives Mary a piece of yarn and directions to put the yarn around the set of eating utensils, Mary *arranges* the yarn so that all the objects are inside the yarn; (3) given two pictures, one of a set of plates and one not a set of plates, Mary *chooses* the picture showing a set of plates; and (4) Mary can *say* an acceptable definition of a set in her own words. Since these behaviors involve more than simple memory and since there are more behaviors involved in this situation, the teacher is much more likely to be correct if she concludes that Mary understands the concept of set. The teacher has increased the certainty that her conclusion (inference) is correct because of the larger number of appropriate behaviors that were observed.

Miss Smith is a regular classroom teacher. She teaches third grade and has consulted Mr. Black, a special educator who functions as a resource teacher in the school, about one of her pupils, Bob, who is having some problems performing tasks in the fine motor coordination area. When Miss Smith originally became concerned about Bob, she had noted that he had difficulty holding a pencil, forming the letters when he was doing handwriting, and cutting with a scissors. As a result of these observations and her suspicion that Bob might have a problem, Miss Smith talked with Mr. Black and asked for his advice.

Mr. Black's job was to serve as a resource for teachers who were experiencing problems such as the one described for Miss Smith and Bob. Mr. Black had some special training in identifying and remediating children's learning problems. Mr. Black suggested some tasks which Miss Smith could administer to Bob in an attempt to decide what kind of problem he had, if any. Here are the observations made by Miss Smith as she administered the tasks: (1) Bob could not *strike* a nail with a hammer; (2) Bob could not stay within the lines when *tracing* through a maze with a pencil; (3) Bob was able to *trace* through the maze with his finger; (4) Bob *told* his teacher he was not pleased with an art project in which he used paint and a paintbrush; (5) on another occasion he *told* the teacher that he was satisfied with an art project in which he used fingerpaints; (6) Bob was not able to *thread* a needle; (7) Bob was sloppy in his *use* of a knife, fork, and spoon; (8) Bob had no difficulty *eating* finger foods; (9) Bob was able to *fold* paper; and (10) Bob was able to *build* block towers. When Miss Smith and Mr. Black considered the behavioral evidence, they were able to discern a pattern.

Were you successful in discovering the pattern in Bob's behavior? Their conclusion was that Bob did have a fine motor coordination problem, but he had a problem only when he was using some kind of tool or implement (hammer, pencil, scissors, paintbrush, eating utensils, etc.). Whenever he was using only his hands in activities such as folding, fingerpainting, tracing, block building, etc., he had no difficulty. As a result of the observations and the inference which was drawn based on the behavioral evidence, Mr. Black helped Miss Smith design a remedial program to help Bob overcome his specific difficulties in the fine motor coordination area.

The major point of the two preceding examples is that instructional decisions should not be based on only one or two small pieces of behavioral evidence. Observations should be continued and decisions withheld until sufficient data have been collected and a reliable pattern of behavior emerges.

PATTERNS OF BEHAVIORS

If we make a habit of collecting essentially the same types of information for each observation, we will have provided ourselves with a standard format and the possibility for patterns of behaviors to emerge will be met. Several variables which are strong contenders for consideration as standard information for each observation are as follows.

The *setting* in which the behavior occurs should be noted. The setting will include such items as what other people were involved in the event, whether any other objects or materials played a prominent role in the situation, what actual peripheral events (other than the central event) may have been occurring, and the time of the performance (including both the date and the time of day). When a teacher is interested in gathering information about a child's typical reactions to a variety of situations, he should be sure to observe the child in a variety of different settings. Different settings are likely to call forth different reactions from the child; and if we did not make our observations in a variety of settings, the information we obtained about that child would probably be somewhat lopsided. Think about the ways you know in which children behave differently on the playground than they do in classroom situations and the point of the previous statement will be quite clear to you.

It may be important to make note of the *stimulus* in the observation process. By this we mean a record should be kept of what triggered or got a behavior started. Then, of course, the *behavior actually performed* or the behaviors displayed by the child will be important to include in the observation. Where indicated, the *sequence* of behaviors exhibited by the learner should be noted. It is frequently important to know the preceding and subsequent behavior surrounding a major behavioral incident.

Time is also a factor to be considered. Some behaviors will be more important at the beginning of a school year, and other behaviors are likely to become more important at other times during the year. For example, when a teacher comes into contact with a new group of children at the beginning of the school year, he often has some written records about the children. He will probably want to check the validity of these records through making observations of children as they typically behave in natural classroom situations. Patterns of behaviors are not likely to become evident in a short span of time. Changes in behaviors over time will indicate growth or lack of progress in various areas of learning. But these changes or patterns of behavior will only be available if records have been kept of the observations over a period of time.

WHO RECORDS OBSERVATIONAL INFORMATION?

So far we have been talking quite a lot about behaviors, processes, and characteristics, and about the business of making inferences. It has been pointed out again and again that behaviors can be observed, whereas processes and characteristics cannot be observed even though they are important.

We have stated that, for our purposes, observation is defined as the process of systematically looking at and recording behavioral information for the purpose of making instructional decisions. Those of you who have taken the time to look up the word *observation* in the dictionary will not be surprised to find that our definition parallels very closely that of the dictionary. As we have said, conclusions are made by drawing inferences on the basis of evidence, and much of the behavioral evidence needed to make these inferences is gathered through systematic observation. Other information-gathering, or assessment, procedures can also be used to gather evidence, and they should be used where they are appropriate, but the fact remains that much of the evidence needed to make inferences is only available through the process of observation. We can only find out whatever it is we need to know by looking at the learner.

The Learner Makes the Record

Some assessment procedures are designed and used so that the individual being studied makes a record of his behaviors for us. Very often the record is made in writing, although there are other ways of making records, such as painting a picture, building a boat, knitting a sweater, making a tape recording, taking a photograph, and so forth. The usual example of an assessment procedure which results in the individual making his own written record is that of a paper and pencil test. When a person answers a test question, he is making a written record of his behavior. We

can then go back again and again and look at his response. The response is generally always available to us for review and reconsideration. Any of these assessment procedures which result in the individual under study making his own record of his behavior are *not* included in our specific definition of observation methods. We should mention, however, that events surrounding and accompanying the written record may be important and will not be available for consideration unless an observer records them while the learner is making his own record. While he is trying to answer test items, another child may be kicking him and thereby negatively influencing his test record. Unless the kicking events are observed and recorded, we would not be aware of them when we evaluate the responses to the test items.

The Observer Makes the Record

Other assessment procedures do not result in the individual under study making his own record of his behavior and are often used in school situations. In these cases, someone else must prepare the record of behavior and this "someone else" is called the observer. When a person gives a speech, or fights with someone else, or offers to share a part of his lunch, or reads orally, or exhibits any of a number of other behaviors, there is no record of behavior to review and reconsider for instructional decision making unless an observer takes the time to prepare that record while the behavior is occurring. In this book we will make a distinction between which assessment procedures are observation methods and which are not observation

methods on the basis of whether the individual produces his own record of behavior. If someone else must watch and make the record, we will think of it as an observation method. In this book, observation is defined as the process of systematically (that is, with a plan) looking at and recording behavior for instructional decision-making purposes. Any method in which the individual prepares his own record is not considered an observation method and is, therefore, outside of our area of concern.

Something Extra

Information should be gathered on all learners as an integral part of teaching, but extra information should be gathered for some pupils. The extra information will be needed for those pupils who are experiencing learning difficulties or who are experiencing other problems which may be interfering with their learning.

Suppose a teacher noticed the following behaviors displayed by a child over a period of time:

Child complains of headaches.

Child has reddish or swollen eyelids.

Child complains of dizziness.

Child is awkward and appears uncoordinated in motor activities.

Child tilts or moves head when performing visual tasks.

Because the behaviors fell into a pattern, the teacher became suspicious that the child might be having a vision problem. (Notice that, up to this point, the teacher had not done anything out of the ordinary in assessing the child. The behaviors listed above had simply been noted during the usual routine teaching activities.) After becoming suspicious about a problem, the teacher performed some extra observations to check out the hunch. Eventually the child was referred to the school nurse, who conducted further tests and made additional referrals in an attempt to get help for the child.

And Now for Some More Examples

Let's consider the area of language development at the preschool level. Below are two lists of behaviors. All of the behaviors in both lists are important components of the process of developing language competence. However, the lists differ in one respect. One list includes behaviors in which the child can be expected to prepare a written record of his behavior as he performs the behavior. The other list includes behaviors in which the child does not make a written record; these are behaviors which must be observed and recorded by someone else as the child performs the behaviors. You will notice that the content involved in each of the parallel statements is highly similar.

Language Behaviors—
Child Makes the Record

1. Given a page of pictures of animals, the child makes an *X* on all of the pictures of horses.

2. After listening to a story, the child draws a picture of his favorite part of the story.

3. The child finds a magazine picture of something red and pastes his picture on a sheet of paper labeled *red.*

4. Child draws lines on his paper to show which objects go together.

5. Given a page of pictures of both foods and animals, the child draws a circle around all the foods.

Language Behaviors—
Observer Makes the Record

1. Given a set of pictures of animals, the child selects all the pictures of horses and groups them together.

2. After listening to a story, the child talks about his favorite part of the story.

3. While paging through a magazine, the child points to red objects.

4. Given sets of colored blocks, the child matches blocks on the basis of color and shape.

5. Given a chart containing pictures of foods and animals, the child points to all the foods.

Let's consider the area of social-emotional development at the primary grade level. We will again present two lists of behavior. All of the behaviors in one list are those for which the child makes his own written record as he performs the behaviors. The other list is of behaviors which are also components of social-emotional development at the primary grade level and is confined to those behaviors which are such that an observer must watch the child and record his behaviors. This example will vary somewhat from the language example in that the items in the two lists are not as parallel.

Social-Emotional Behaviors—
Observer Makes the Record

1. Child stands in line waiting for a turn at the drinking fountain on the playground.

Social-Emotional Behaviors—
Child Makes the Record

1. Given a test paper, the child scribbles on it and writes "I hate tests."

Language Behaviors— *Child Makes the Record*	Language Behaviors— *Observer Makes the Record*
2. When told by the teacher that he cannot behave in a certain way, child cries.	2. Child writes a poem about feeling excited at the circus.
3. Child plays tag, an interactive game, according to the rules.	3. Child completes a book interest inventory by marking the titles of books he's interested in reading.
4. When another child startles him by putting a rubber spider on his arm, child jumps away and screams.	4. Child writes about an idea for a class party for the suggestion box.
5. Child says "Please" when requesting something from another child.	5. Given some open-ended sentences, child completes the sentences to tell how he feels in different situations.

Observation as a Supplement to Other Information

Sometimes, when information which forms the base for instructional decisions is gathered by means other than observational methods, we may become interested in gathering additional data to supplement the original information. Suppose, for example, that we have a paper prepared by a learner which is his written record of the first five letters of the alphabet. Suppose that we are not pleased with what we see on that paper since he has not formulated these five letters very adequately. In this case, supplementary information might be gained by observing the learner while he is actually forming these five letters of the alphabet. Through this use of observation, information about his difficulties might be obtained which can then be used to make appropriate instructional decisions with the ultimate result that the child improves his performance.

Teachers often fall into the trap of evaluating only certain types of learning. As you might expect, the types of learning that are evaluated most frequently are those which are the easiest to assess. That is why teachers are generally able to produce quite a lot of information about how children perform on tests, but are frequently not able to produce information about children's behaviors in areas such as social interactions, behaviors on the playground, oral reading situations, and their behaviors in a variety of other nontest situations. In order to make a variety of necessary instructional decisions, comprehensive information is needed about learners, and comprehensive information is possible only when a variety of assessment procedures are used. This means that we will need to use both observational and nonobservational methods of gathering information in order to provide a complete picture of the learner.

The fifth grade teacher, Mrs. Jones, was sure that Harry had a reading problem. However, she was not sure about the exact nature of the reading problem. Mrs. Jones had already given Harry a variety of reading tasks, like tests, to which he responded in written form. Mrs. Jones hesitated to develop a remedial program for Harry until she had more information. Here are brief descriptions of some of Mrs. Jones' activities intended to extend her information about Harry's reading difficulties.

Mrs. Jones had collected some data about Harry's skills in phonic analysis and found that he could perform only a few of the simplest skills in phonic analysis when he was given written or pictorial tasks. She supplemented this information about phonic analysis skills by observing and recording Harry's behavior as he responded to some tasks requiring oral behaviors. For example, she asked Harry to produce some beginning consonant sounds and noted his behavior. She also observed the placement of Harry's articulators (tongue, lips, teeth, etc.) as he attempted to model her production of some consonants.

Mrs. Jones also knew that Harry did not respond correctly when he was given a paragraph to read and then expected to select the correct answers to a series of comprehension questions about the content of the paragraph. She wanted to know if Harry had the thinking skills in his repertoire and was unable to demonstrate them because of his reading problem or if he had not attained the thinking skills as well as the reading skills. To check this, Mrs. Jones orally read some paragraphs to Harry. She then recorded Harry's behaviors as he responded orally to some comprehension questions she asked him. As a result of supplementing her information about Harry's reading behaviors in these and other ways, Mrs. Jones was able to obtain a more complete description of Harry's problem and was, therefore, better able to design a remedial program which was likely to be successful.

Some Examples

We have said that some behaviors, especially those which indicate the process of application, can only be known through the use of observation methods. How else could you gather information about the child's sharing a toy? You couldn't give him a test. How else could you assess a child's skipping? You couldn't give him a test. How else could you find out if a child eats popcorn? You couldn't give him a test.

Here are some examples, from the field of science at the intermediate grade level, to further illustrate this point. As you consider these examples, check to see if

you agree with our position that these are behaviors which require the use of observation for assessment. Could you use a paper and pencil test to determine these behaviors?

Science—Behaviors Requiring Observation

1. On a nature walk, the learner can find leaves from the oak, elm, and maple trees.
2. The learner can focus the microscope properly.
3. The learner contributes a wild flower specimen to the class collection.
4. The learner conducts an experiment demonstrating static electricity.
5. The learner feeds the gerbil daily without reminders.

In the preceding discussion of the teacher's overall instructional decision-making responsibilities, we suggested that observation can and should be used to supplement the information that had been gathered using other data-gathering methods, such as tests.

Need Comprehensive Information

Since some behaviors are such that the learner makes his own written record and other behaviors are such that an observer must make the record, it follows that both observational and nonobservational methods must be used in order to have comprehensive information about a learner's behaviors.

Let's consider some information about Sarah, a nine-year-old girl with learning problems who was placed temporarily in a resource room while a special educator conducted intensive educational diagnoses, and formulated and field tested a prescriptive program. This validated prescriptive program was forwarded to the regular fourth grade teacher when Sarah returned to her regular class placement. Consider the differences, that might have resulted in the prescriptive program for Sarah, between a set of limited information (A) and a set of comprehensive information (B).

A. Limited Information–Reading Behaviors

1. Given a series of fifty flashcards of vocabulary words at the second grade level, Sarah pronounces only 10 percent of the words correctly.
2. Given pictures of single objects and several objects and associated vocabulary words (*ball, balls*), Sarah cannot state the generalization about plurals.
3. Sarah cannot orally read simple sentences from a basal reader for the first grade.
4. When listening to pairs of words, some of which are the same and some of which are different, Sarah cannot state which pairs are the same and which are different.
5. After listening to a sentence read orally by the teacher, Sarah cannot find a picture to match the sentence from a collection of pictures.

B. Comprehensive Information–
Reading Behaviors Plus Social-Emotional Behaviors

To the list of Sarah's reading behaviors, let's add these social-emotional behaviors:

1. When sitting with a group of children during story time, Sarah "bothers" other children by touching, poking, talking, kicking, and so on.
2. When her desk is moved away from others, Sarah draws a picture; she attends to this task for five minutes.
3. When a member of a small reading group, Sarah's reaction when another child reads orally is to turn around in her chair and look out the window.
4. When asked to collect some papers from other children, Sarah refuses by stamping her foot and saying, "No!"

5. When an adult sits with her and immediately rewards her appropriate behaviors with raisins, Sarah attends to reading tasks for at least ten minutes.

Utilizing the set of comprehensive information, one important conclusion pertinent to formulating the prescriptive program emerged: Sarah appeared to be unable to function in group situations for academic learning tasks; therefore, the prescriptive program was designed so that Sarah would be instructed on an individual basis.

OBSERVATION FOR DECISIONS ABOUT
IDENTIFYING CHARACTERISTICS OF LEARNERS

Many instructional decisions depend upon identification of relevant characteristics of learners. Almost everyone is aware of the fact that before we can begin in teaching, we must have some idea of what it is we want the learner to learn. We must know what we want the learner to be able to do, or how we want him to be able to behave, as the result of the instruction which we provide for him. You will quickly recognize that this involves the formulation of instructional objectives for learners. How does a teacher know which instructional objective to formulate for any given learner or group of learners at any given time? The answer is that the teacher must base his decision on some information about the learner's past performances. Of course, much of the information needed here will have been gathered using observation methods.

Making Instructional Decisions About Entry Behaviors

We call the behaviors that a learner brings with him to a new learning situation *entry behaviors.* In other words, he enters a new situation with certain behaviors already in his repertoire. Teachers need to know which entry behaviors are held by a learner so that they are not incorrectly formulating instructional objectives. Thus, the major purpose of observation related to entry behaviors is to help the teacher establish the current level of functioning of a child. Once that level has been determined, the task of deciding what to instruct and where to begin instruction is made much easier. Observation related to entry behaviors has a much different function than observation related to evaluating achievement. The purpose of assessing entry behaviors is to determine where to start instruction whereas the purpose of assessing achievement is to evaluate effectiveness of instruction.

Observing for the purpose of determining entry behaviors, then, helps the teacher avoid the trap of formulating objectives which are inappropriate for a given child. Instructional objectives could be inappropriate in two ways. If the learner already has a behavior in his repertoire, then he is quite likely to be disinterested or bored with the whole process of learning if he is expected to participate in instruction for something he has already mastered. If, on the other hand, the teacher has specified an objective which is beyond the entry behaviors of the learner, the learner may find himself frustrated in being expected to achieve a goal which is too difficult or complex for him at a particular stage of his development.

Making Instructional Decisions
Related to Individualizing Instruction

The learner's past performances under different teaching procedures and instructional materials must also be determined in order to plan appropriate teaching procedures and to select appropriate materials for the learner. Those of you who are reading between the lines will quickly recognize that this previous statement is highly related to individualization of instruction. It is known that some learners respond better to some teaching methods and instructional materials than they do to others. Some people prefer to listen to information rather than to read about it, for example. Some people learn better when manipulative materials are used, while others perform better when verbal methods are used. If a teacher has been able to collect information about a learner's history of successes with different instructional materials, then the teacher is better able to select appropriate teaching methods and materials which can be used with some assurance of effectiveness with the learner.

As teachers focus on collecting information for the purpose of identifying relevant characteristics of learners, they are quite likely to turn up bits and pieces of information about the learner which will cause them to become somewhat suspicious about the learner's performance in a particular area. When teachers are in the habit of continually monitoring information about children, they are very often able to detect the beginnings of learning problems very early. In general, the earlier a problem can be detected and identified, the easier it is to do something about the problem. In this respect, teachers can engage in preventive action—by detecting and attending to minor problems early, the development of serious problems can probably be prevented.

Task Analysis

One of the important purposes for observation is the assessment and identification of relevant characteristics of learners—task analysis is one method of identifying these characteristics. Task analysis, which might be used to provide guidelines regarding *which* behaviors should be assessed, requires that entry behaviors, or prerequisite skills, be identified and that the sequence of behaviors required to perform a task be identified. Task analysis may be used as the basis for diagnosing learners' needs and also for sequencing a series of behavioral objectives. In diagnosis, it is necessary to trace backwards until we find the behavior in the sequence the child can perform and then to begin taking him forward from there.

A task analysis for dialing the telephone might look like this:

Task Analysis for Dialing the Telephone

The task: The learner will be able to dial a given number on a telephone without making errors and without assistance.

Steps in the task:

1. Can recognize numerals *0-9*

2. Can recognize alphabet letters *A-Z*

3. Can differentiate between left and right direction

4. Can pick up receiver and demonstrate how to hold it

5. Can point to the dial and show how to put fingers in holes

6. Can point to the stopper

7. Can turn the dial with his finger until it is stopped by the stopper

8. Can put his finger in the hole matching a number he is given and move his finger to the stopper (he has dialed one number)

9. Can dial two numbers in proper order when he is given the two numbers

10. Can dial more and more numbers in the proper order until he has dialed all seven numbers in a given telephone number

11. Can repeat step 8 while holding the receiver to his ear

12. Can repeat steps 9 and 10 while holding the receiver to his ear

13. Can repeat step 12 going in correct left-to-right order when he is given a written number

Some More Examples

We have described a teacher's need to identify learners' characteristics in order to select appropriate objectives, methods, and materials for instruction. Here is an example from the area of mathematics at the intermediate grade level. When a teacher assesses the behaviors already accomplished by learners, he is determining the entry behaviors of learners. If a teacher knows that the learner can divide, he might decide on a new objective of expecting the learner to check or prove the accuracy of his solutions to division problems. Since the objective is dependent on multiplication skills, however, the teacher must also determine if the learner has a set of entry behaviors in the area of multiplication. If he does not, then the teacher's expectation would be inappropriate; if he does, then the objective appears to be appropriate.

Here's another similar example in the area of language development at the primary grade level. Let's suppose that a teacher decided that a certain group of second graders would accomplish the following language behaviors or objectives:

1. Given two simple sentences, a child can restate them as a compound sentence.

2. Given a picture, a child can formulate and state a sentence describing the picture.

3. A child can dictate a short story about his experiences on a nature walk.

4. A child can consult his personal picture dictionary to determine the correct spelling of words he wishes to use in a short, written composition about winter.

Now these objectives may or may not be appropriate for these learners. If, for example, a child did not know any conjunctions, then the first objective might have been inappropriate. If the child did not know what a sentence was, then objective 2 was an unreasonable expectation. For objective 3 the child needed to be able to tell a story (to have learned the concept of "story") and know appropriate vocabulary about what he saw on the nature walk to satisfactorily accomplish the objective. The child needed to have mastered a whole set of dictionary skills in order for the teacher to consider objective 4 appropriate.

What we are saying here is that the teacher must be able to analyze a task (the behavioral objective really describes a task for the learner) to determine and sequence its subparts. And *then* the teacher must determine if the child has attained the learning level required by the subparts for the behaviors he is expected to perform to be considered reasonable.

Early Detection of Problems

When teachers are attuned to detecting and identifying the relevant characteristics of learners, they place themselves in an ideal position for becoming aware of conditions in learning which may result in learning problems. In addition to helping teachers discern learners' problems, being knowledgeable about the specific behaviors of learners enables teachers to decide on appropriate objectives, methods, and materials. When the strategy of early detection is followed, learning problems can usually be identified early enough so that teachers can design ameliorative procedures that, with greater assurance, will be successful.

For example, a teacher might become alerted to the existence of a vision problem when he considers these and other similar behaviors exhibited by a preschool child in the areas of mathematics and gross motor development:

1. A child cannot hit a target when throwing a beanbag at distances of 5, 10, or 15 feet.
2. A child frequently bumps into chairs, tables, blocks, etc., when walking around the classroom.
3. He cannot walk heel-to-toe fashion on a line drawn on the floor.
4. When shown two pictures on a chart placed several feet away, the child cannot tell which picture shows more objects.
5. The child cannot name a numeral which the teacher has printed on the chalkboard.
6. The child complains of a headache during an activity in which he is expected to draw three circles on his paper.

In summary, observation plays a critical role in making instructional decisions related to educational characteristics of children. Teachers need to use observation to identify the relevant characteristics of children so they can make decisions about selecting appropriate objectives, methods, and materials for instruction.

EVALUATING ACHIEVEMENT

Another somewhat specific purpose for using observation methods is to use observation to evaluate the learner's achievement of objectives. It is not enough to take the time to specify a behavioral objective, and to carefully think through and plan the instructional method and the material for the learner, if the same amount of care and attention is not then given to a careful look at the learner's performance as the result of the teaching. We need to know whether or not the learner is able to exhibit the behavior that was expected of him in the objective. If the objective said he should be able to correctly pronounce five words, then we need to know if he pronounced the five words correctly. If the objective stated he would be able to climb a rope ladder in two minutes, then we need to know if he climbed the ladder in the specified amount of time. And if the objective said that he would spontaneously converse with another child during a free play activity, then we need to know whether or not this conversation did indeed take place during the play period.

Furthermore, using observation methods to evaluate achievement should help the teacher make important decisions about future instructional strategies. If observation reveals that a learner has reached a given objective after he has been exposed to a certain instructional method, the teacher might very well decide to use the same method to help the child reach the next related objective. On the other hand, careful observation of a child's attempts to reach a certain objective should help the teacher decide what alternative strategy might be tried.

Application of Skills and Understandings

Many of the objectives of instruction involve the application of learned skills and concepts to everyday situations. In these instances, observation methods are the most appropriate procedures to be used in determining whether or not the behaviors specified in the objective have been displayed by the learner. It is one thing to answer a test question about the importance of good manners on the highway, but it is quite another thing to actually display these manners in highway driving situations. The same is true for many of the objectives formulated for learners in school situations. It is quite possible for learners to verbalize some idea, as they often do in a test, but very often when the idea is applied to a real-life situation, we find that the learner cannot translate the idea into behavior. The only way we can find out that the learner can or cannot apply an idea to a real situation, in many instances, is to observe his performance in the situation and record the results.

Some objectives are such that the behavior included in the objective is of a type in which the learner does not prepare his own record of that behavior. Learners do not prepare written records when they dramatize a new vocabulary word, orally count a set of objects, play a game, climb a tree, recite a poem, or throw a ball. In these cases (and there are thousands and thousands of them occurring all the time in all school situations), observation is the only appropriate procedure for obtaining information about achievement of the objectives. It is impossible to be an instructional decision maker without using observation on a daily basis. We need to watch the learner as he performs and record the behaviors he displays in order to determine whether he has attained the objective.

A most important generalization has been alluded to in the preceding statements: the most valid information-gathering procedure is the one which allows the most direct display of the behavior. If we want to know about oral reading skills, then we should observe the child while he reads orally. If we want to know about the motor skills of jumping and hopping, then we should observe the child as he jumps and hops, and so on.

Progress May Be Slow

Notice that we have been talking about evaluating the learner's achievement of behavioral objectives. Behavioral objectives are usually formulated so that very small increments of progress in learning are incorporated within the objectives. Many, many behaviors need to be displayed before some real indication of progress is noticeable. Day-to-day improvement in learners, in reading or arithmetic or any other area, is generally evidenced by very small gains. Very often these gains are not noticed unless adequate records are kept and the pattern of behavior change over a period of time is studied. If the behaviors are of a type that requires evaluation by observation methods, then the records of the observation will need to be reviewed periodically to adequately assess changes and improvements in learners.

Checking for Transfer

Observation represents one of the most effective means of gathering information about those kinds of behaviors which we expect learners to transfer or apply to everyday situations. This is true because observation usually allows the learner to perform without being interrupted or distracted, and it allows the observer the opportunity to be unobtrusive and objective in his record-keeping. It is quite possible that a large portion of the time when he is being observed, he may not be aware that he is being "tested" and watched for purposes of gathering information about his behavior. Many other assessment procedures do not afford this possibility of detachment. For example, when we give a child a paper and pencil test, he is very much aware of the fact that he is being assessed.

One of the situations in which teachers experience recurring problems related to transfer of learning is in speech improvement or therapy. Oftentimes, a speech therapist will work with the individual child one or several times during the week. While with the therapist, the child often performs admirably, but when he is observed speaking within the regular classroom situation, he often reverts to previous speech patterns. When the regular classroom teacher is aware of what the child is reported to have learned in his speech therapy sessions, the teacher can monitor these classroom speech patterns and feed back to the therapist information about the child's inability to transfer what he has learned. The therapist, in turn, may make different instructional decisions based on this knowledge of the amount of transfer.

And Now for a Few Examples

There should be a direct relationship between the behavior specified in the objective and the behavior called forth in the evaluation procedure used to determine if the learner has achieved the objective. Let's see how this principle works by looking at some objectives and some evaluation procedures in the area of fine motor skills at the preschool level.

Objective	*Evaluation Procedure*
1. Given two small containers and a small block, the child can dump the block from one container to the other five times in a row without spilling the block.	1. The teacher gives the child two containers and one block. The teacher places the block in one of the containers and tells the child to dump the block back and forth from one container to the other five times without spilling the block. If he does the task five times, the child achieves the objective.

Objective	*Evaluation Procedure*
2. Given five small blocks, the child can build a tower successfully in two trials.	2. The teacher gives the child a pile of five small blocks and tells the child to build a tower using all five blocks. If the child is successful on the first or second trial, he achieves the objective.
3. Given a model of a circle, the child draws a circle on his paper—the line making a circle must be curved and closed.	3. The teacher gives the child a piece of paper and shows him a card with a circle drawn on it. The child is directed to make a circle like the model. If his circle meets the criteria of using a curved line and being closed, he achieves the objective.

Many of the important general objectives of instruction involve the learner's process of applying what he has learned to natural or real-life situations. Very often, observation methods must be used to determine if learners have achieved these application-type objectives. One teacher formulated some objectives, in the area of mathematics, which were related to transferring and applying computation skills in addition and subtraction to simulated, real-life purchasing situations. A list of some of these objectives follows. Note that the behaviors in the objectives are such that an observer can record whether specific behaviors are exhibited by the learners.

1. When playing the role of shopper, the learner will give the storekeeper the correct amount of money to buy two items.
2. When playing the role of storekeeper, the learner will total the amount of money he owes.
3. When playing the role of storekeeper, and given too much money by another child for his purchase, the learner will give correct change.
4. When giving the storekeeper too much money for his purchase and receiving change, the learner playing the role of the shopper will check his change and tell if he received the correct amount.

TEACHER BEHAVIOR

The behaviors of learners and the behaviors of the teacher are inextricably intertwined. Just as it is important to monitor the behaviors of learners as they make progress toward objectives, it is also important for the teacher to monitor his behaviors and to analyze the relationship between his behaviors and his learners' behaviors. Let's consider a brief example in the area of social-emotional behavior at the intermediate grade level.

A certain fourth grader, Robert, consistently bumps, jostles, pokes and exhibits other similar "bothering" behaviors toward other learners as he moves about the classroom. Each time he somehow bothered another learner, the teacher said, "Don't do that, Robert," or made some other similar verbal statement. When the teacher recorded his own behavior in relation to Robert's behavior, he quickly noted both a possible cause and a solution for Robert's behavior pattern. The teacher concluded that his attention (making verbal statements) might be reinforcing Robert's behavior, therefore maintaining it at a high level of frequency (see left portion of the graph in Figure 1-1). The solution was to withdraw the probable reinforcer (verbal statements) and ignore Robert's "bothering" behaviors whenever possible.

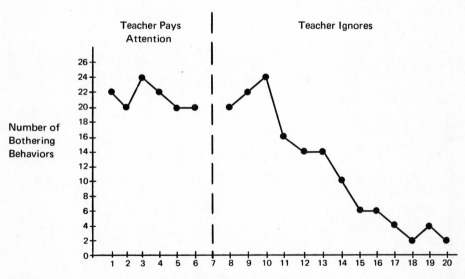

FIGURE 1-1 Robert's "bothering" behaviors

In order to determine if the solution worked, the teacher continued to record both his own and Robert's behavior over a period of time. He found that if he ignored Robert's bumping and jostling, the child's disruptive behaviors decreased (see right portion of the graph in Figure 1-1).

Such an example should demonstrate that it is highly desirable for teachers to devise means of observing their own behavior. This can be easily accomplished through the use of videotape recordings. Usually the teacher himself need not be concerned with the technicalities of obtaining such recordings. However, he will need to think about the *purpose* of observing his own behavior. He should be interested in checking the extent to which he actually performs the roles he thinks he does. In this situation, the need to determine a relationship or comparison between his expected behavior and his actual behavior will define the purpose for this self-observation and determine just what to observe as he views himself on the videotape. Of course, two or more teachers might want to cooperate by taking turns observing each other's teaching and providing feedback to each other.

BUT I'M NOT A TEACHER!

The focus of this chapter has been on the kinds of instructional decisions that classroom teachers must make and the need to use observation techniques as the basis for many of these decisions. But what about the nonteacher who is interested in observation methods? Very often nonteaching observers are sent into classroom situations. What is their purpose and what do they observe? Let's consider several purposes, guidelines in themselves, and provide suggestions as to what might be observed in light of these purposes.

Preservice Teachers

If the observer is a teacher trainee, he will probably want to do several things during his observation. For some of his observation time at least, he will want to play the role of the teacher. In this role, he will imagine that he is responsible for making instructional decisions and he will be using observation methods just as if he were the teacher. In this situation, the nonteaching observer would be functioning the same as an inservice teacher-observer functions in the classroom. The preservice teacher-observer might also use his observations to determine the types of behaviors expected of teachers. In other words, he would be observing in order to determine what the role of the teacher is and what instructional decisions need to be made daily by the teacher. In this regard, he might need to make observations about the setting within which teaching occurs, the characteristics of the learners for whom a teacher is responsible, and information about the roles of the other professionals with whom a teacher comes into contact.

Research

Sometimes observers are present in classroom situations for purposes of research and evaluation, the research questions to be answered providing the guidelines for the observation. For example, suppose a teacher is expected to implement a particular model program. Later, the behavior and performance of the children in this model program will be compared with those from children in a different program in order to ascertain the relative effectiveness of each. In order for the research study to yield results which can be interpreted later, it would be necessary to determine that each of the teachers is indeed performing as the model program dictates. A researcher-observer then might be sent into the classroom to verify that the teacher is performing behaviors in accordance with the dictates of a particular model program.

Diagnosis

At other times observers might be sent into classroom situations to add to the available diagnostic information on a particular learner. It may be that the classroom teacher, having exhausted his resources as an information-gatherer, still has not determined the cause of a learning difficulty a child is experiencing and is unable to make appropriate instructional decisions for that child. In this case, a resource person (such as a school psychologist, special educator, nurse, speech therapist, or any of the resource professionals available to schools) might be called in to make specialized observations of the child in the classroom situation in order to determine the best course of action for that child. Since it will be incumbent upon these diagnosticians to obtain an accurate report about the child, a carefully planned observation method is a necessity.

Parents

Parents may also be observers in the classroom. Whatever the possible reasons for parents being present, they should be aware of their purpose for making an observation, since the purpose will provide guidelines about what and how to observe. Perhaps a child is experiencing a problem and his parents remain unconvinced of his difficulty. Having agreed that children are likely to behave differently in school than at home, the parents might have expressed a desire to "see for themselves." In this case, having the parents observe their child in the school situation might help convince them of the veracity of the information previously given to them about the child, by the teacher or by some other professional. Another possibility is that the teacher may have worked out a special prescriptive teaching program for a child and the cooperation of the parents in extending the program to the home is being elicited. As part of their training to take over the teaching program at home, parents may have come to the classroom to observe the teacher, the learner, and the method in order to determine what needs to be done, how it is to be done, and what the typical reaction of the child is likely to be.

SUMMARY

This chapter included a rationale for using observation methods based on the principle that inferences about the characteristics of learners must be based on observable evidence. Observation was defined as the process of systematically looking at and recording behavior for instructional decision-making purposes. The distinction between observation methods and other assessment procedures was made on the basis of whether the learner makes the written record of his behavior (such as on a test, not an observation method) or whether the behavior exhibited by the learner is such that an observer must prepare the written record (an observation method).

The teacher was described as an instructional decision maker who needs evidence upon which to make decisions. Discussion centered around the ways in which information gathered through observation would be used in making a variety of instructional decisions.

ACTIVITY 1

Here's an activity which will allow you to gain some initial experience in the use of observation methods even though you may not yet have been exposed to the intricacies involved in observation. This activity—and the use of the observation forms on pages 35-43—will give you practice in drawing inferences from behavioral information. Here's how to proceed:

1. Choose a learner—any learner—but we want you to focus your attention on just one learner for now.

2. Choose an activity which occurs daily and decide to concentrate your observations on that activity—for example, free play, recess, reading, or project work.

3. Complete the forms on pages 35-43 as you observe the learner in the activity for *five consecutive days*.

4. After collection of the observational data has been completed, use the information and draw a conclusion about the performance of the learner in the activity. (Record your conclusion in writing so you won't be changing your mind later.)

5. Next, show your observational records to a colleague and ask him to draw a conclusion about the learner on the basis of your behavioral data. Ask him to record his conclusion in writing so he can't change his mind.

6. Finally, compare your conclusion with your colleague's. If you disagree substantially, discuss your disagreements and attempt to validate the different conclusions through further observation.

ACTIVITY 2

Here's an experience which should help sharpen your understanding of how instructional decisions are based on disciplined observation.

1. Identify an area in which you think a teacher could improve his instructional decision making.

2. Using observation methods, collect data relevant to the instructional decision you've chosen to investigate.

3. Show your observation records to a colleague and describe to him how the instructional decision making could be improved using the information you gathered.

4 5-minute period

Observation No. _____

*Observer:*_____   *Date:*_____

                                              Time: from_____ to _____

*Learner's Name:*_____

Grade: _____   *Activity:*_____

Describe, in behavioral terms, the setting within which the activity typically takes place.

_____

_____

_____

_____

List all the behaviors displayed by the learner during a ten-minute period in which he is engaged (or supposed to be engaged) in the chosen activity. If the same behavior occurs more than once, indicate this by making tallies in the frequency column.

Description of Behavior   **Frequency**

_____

_____

_____

_____

_____

_____

_____

_____

_____

_____

_____

_____

_____

*Observer:*_____   *Date:*_____

                                         Time: from_____ to _____

*Learner's Name:*_____

Grade: _____ *Activity:*_____

Describe, in behavioral terms, the setting within which the activity typically takes place.

_____

_____

_____

_____

List all the behaviors displayed by the learner during a ten-minute period in which he is engaged (or supposed to be engaged) in the chosen activity. If the same behavior occurs more than once, indicate this by making tallies in the frequency column.

Description of Behavior   **Frequency**

_____

_____

_____

_____

_____

_____

_____

_____

_____

_____

_____

_____

_____

Observation No. _____

Observer: _____   *Date:* _____

                                                  Time: from _____ *to* _____

Learner's Name: _____

Grade: _____   *Activity:* _____

Describe, in behavioral terms, the setting within which the activity typically takes place.

_____

_____

_____

_____

List all the behaviors displayed by the learner during a ten-minute period in which he is engaged (or supposed to be engaged) in the chosen activity. If the same behavior occurs more than once, indicate this by making tallies in the frequency column.

Description of Behavior   **Frequency**

_____

_____

_____

_____

_____

_____

_____

_____

_____

_____

_____

_____

_____

Observation No. _____

Observer:_____   Date:_____

Time: from_____ to _____

Learner's Name:_____

Grade: _____ Activity:_____

Describe, in behavioral terms, the setting within which the activity typically takes place.

_____

_____

_____

_____

List all the behaviors displayed by the learner during a ten-minute period in which he is engaged (or supposed to be engaged) in the chosen activity. If the same behavior occurs more than once, indicate this by making tallies in the frequency column.

Description of Behavior   **Frequency**

_____

_____

_____

_____

_____

_____

_____

_____

_____

_____

_____

_____

_____

_____

Observation No. _____

Observer: _____   *Date:* _____

                                    Time: from _____ *to* _____

Learner's Name: _____

Grade: _____   *Activity:* _____

Describe, in behavioral terms, the setting within which the activity typically takes place.

_____

_____

_____

_____

List all the behaviors displayed by the learner during a ten-minute period in which he is engaged (or supposed to be engaged) in the chosen activity. If the same behavior occurs more than once, indicate this by making tallies in the frequency column.

Description of Behavior   **Frequency**

_____

_____

_____

_____

_____

_____

_____

_____

_____

_____

_____

_____

_____

TWO

Methods of observing
and record keeping

Probably any information of interest to a teacher can be obtained through observation—but that is not the point. The point is to use observation when and only when a definite purpose has been determined for gathering information about the learner—and observation methods are suited to that purpose. Some assessment procedures, such as paper and pencil tests, are really better information-gathering devices for some purposes than are observation methods. However, there remain a great number and diversity of behaviors which can only be assessed via observation methods. Some examples of situations which require the use of observation methods are oral speaking, listening skills, oral reading, performing experiments, drawing, playing musical instruments, playing games, using equipment, social interactions, craft activities, working cooperatively on group projects, most of the motor skills typically included in the physical education program, and handwriting. And we've named only a few!

   Given the variety of school situations requiring instructional decisions, the teacher will need various information-gathering observation methods and tools. Different types of information will require the use of different recording forms. Regardless of the purpose of the observation and the type of record that is to be used, there are several general procedures to be followed which comprise a method of observing. This chapter is a presentation of the general principles involved in all types of observations.

When you complete this chapter and the recommended activities, you should be able to:

1. List, in sequence, the four major steps which constitute a method of observation
2. Prepare operational definitions for the behaviors you want to observe
3. Decide what type of record form to use when given different purposes for observing
4. Check for agreement between observers who observe the same child for same purpose
5. Recognize sources of error likely to arise in observation situations
6. Conduct observations using the four major steps given in the chapter

THE IMPLICATIONS OF "PURPOSE" IN OBSERVATION

The first step in the process of observation is to determine the purpose. As was pointed out in Chapter One, the purposes for observation will vary depending on the orientation of the observer. If the observer is a teacher, the instructional decision to be made forms the purpose. If the observer is a researcher, the questions under investigation form the purpose. An aspiring teacher's purpose might be to determine how teachers behave, what events take place in classrooms, how learners of different ages behave, and so on.

The Purpose Is the Key

The observer should be thoroughly informed about the purpose underlying the observation before attempting the observation and making the record. If the purpose is well defined, it will dictate the following guidelines for the procedure:

1. Who will make the observation.
2. Who or what will be observed.
3. Where the observation will take place (there should be a variety of situations included).
4. When the observation will occur (there should be diversified time periods).
5. How the observation will be recorded.

Here's an Example

Let's consider several different types of instructional decisions that might be required and see what effects different purposes have on the observation process. Usually, these effects will reveal themselves in terms of a determination about what to observe and how to record the observation. For example, a teacher might be interested in how often he is using verbal statements of reward (the purpose). With regard to what will be included in the observation, the most crucial aspect will be to define what is meant by "verbal statement of reward" so that the observer will know exactly when the teacher is making such a statement and when he is not. In other words, it will be necessary to define operationally what is meant by an *instance of the behavior* or event under study.

In the case of this example, we might define an instance of the behavior as any time the teacher says something indicating a child, or children, performed correctly or behaved positively. Therefore, when the teacher says, "Great job on that wooden boat you're building, Tom!" the observer would tally it as an instance of the event "verbal statement of a reward." On the other hand, if the teacher smiles at a child, it would not be recorded as an occurrence of the event "verbal statement of a reward" since the behavior was not verbal (although it may have been rewarding to the child who was the recipient of the smile).

Since it is the teacher's behavior that is to be observed, it will be necessary to enlist the cooperation of some other person to make the observation and to record the observations. Since the type of behavior of interest is one which is likely to occur many times during the day and in all situations during the day, a time sampling procedure will probably be needed. This means that several time periods throughout the day would be chosen arbitrarily as ones during which the observation would take place, and the time periods would be chosen so that a representative sampling of classroom activities would be involved in the observations. For example, five-minute periods, beginning on the hour and on the half hour, could be used.

Given that this observation's purpose is to determine the amount of verbal statements of reward being dispensed by the teacher, a behavior tallying procedure would be the best type of record to use. A sample observation guide, which summarizes information about the observation, is shown on page 48. After the observation has been conducted for a week, the resulting tallies could be converted to a graph such as the one shown in Figure 2-1. Notice that the graph tells *what* happened but does not indicate *why* there were considerably more verbal statements of rewards given on Friday than on any of the previous four days. However, an observational record of the events surrounding the dispensing of the reward

Where: <u>*Classroom 103*</u>

When: <u>*10:00 – 10:10 a.m. daily*</u>

What: <u>*Number of verbal statements of reward*</u>

Who: <u>*Mrs. Smith (classroom teacher)*</u>

How: <u>*Tallies on 3 x 5 card*</u>

statement would probably allow us to make an *inference* about the causes of the pattern.

More Examples

Let's take another very different type of situation for contrast and see what effect the purpose for the observation has on the manner in which the observation is conducted. Suppose that a teacher needs to make a decision about whether to recommend a child for a special summer music, dance, and drama program. For this

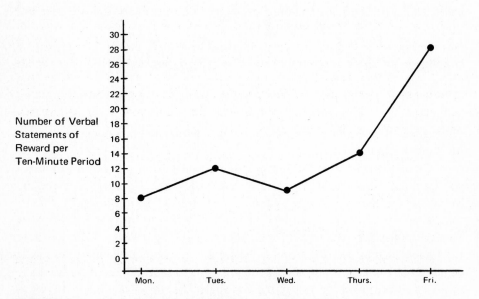

FIGURE 2-1   Verbal reward given during a one-week period

Sample Items from Rating Scale

1. To what extent does the child pursue music activities independently?

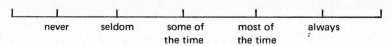

    never   seldom   some of   most of   always
                       the time   the time

2. To what extent does the child pursue dance activities independently?

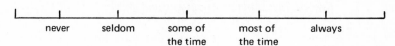

    never   seldom   some of   most of   always
                       the time   the time

3. To what extent does the child pursue drama activities independently?

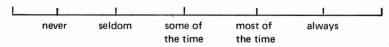

    never   seldom   some of   most of   always
                       the time   the time

purpose, it will be necessary to identify all those behaviors (or as many as possible) related to the areas of music, dance, and drama which the child performs and to give some indication of the frequency and quality of the behaviors. To achieve this purpose, it will be necessary to develop and use a rating scale like the one shown on this page. When and where to observe are considerations that will be handled by using the rating scale whenever and wherever the child will be performing the behaviors listed on the rating scale—whatever those might be. Since the teacher will be available and since it is usually more efficient for the teacher to make the observation than to bring in some outside observer, the teacher will be the observer.

A rating scale, well suited to the purpose of the observation (as described above), is but one among many means of recording what is observed. The following is a brief list of contrasting instructional decisions, and purposes, behaviors observed and methods of recording data:

Instructional decision: To determine what math materials a child uses spontaneously during independent activities

What to observe: Instances of math materials handled by the child during independent activity times

Record form: Checklist

Instructional decision: To determine how to group some children for a social studies project activity so that each group has at least one child who can function as a leader

What to observe:	Instances of leadership behavior among the children
Record form:	Anecdotal records
Instructional decision:	To determine if the inappropriate behavior of thumb sucking, which has concerned a child's mother in the home situation, is occurring at school
What to observe:	Instances of thumb sucking
Record form:	Behavior tallying and charting

TYPES OF RECORDS

We have seen that the purpose for observing must be determined first since it, in turn, determines what will be observed and since a host of other decisions are made based on the purpose. Decisions about the type of record to be used for the observation should be made next—along with actually developing and designing the form. As you have seen in the previous examples, there is a variety of records that can be utilized with observation methods. Again, the purpose of making the observation can be used as a guideline in determining the type of record to use.

The basic types of records available to an observer are anecdotal records, participation charts, checklists, rating scales, and behavior tallying and charting procedures. The remaining chapters in this book cover these specific types of records and the fine points of developing and using each of them. Slight variations and modifications of each of these basic types of records exist. We will not be concerned with compiling an exhaustive description of possible variations; rather we will concern ourselves with providing information about these basic types of record forms and leave the variations on the basic theme to your imagination.

Records Depend on Purpose

The decision about which of the types of records to use at any given time must be made on the basis of the instructional decision which is to be made using the observational data or the purpose for the observation. Because of the different characteristics of various records, we will find that certain types of records match well with some instructional decisions and not with others. As each of the types of records are presented in later chapters, you will be apprised of the types of instructional decisions and purposes best matched to the particular record.

Some types of records are easier to use and result in more objective and reliable information than other records. In the final analysis, however, if the type of record chosen is not matched to the purpose for the observation, the choice of record form is inappropriate no matter how objective and usable it may be. For example, you will see later that checklists are relatively easy to use and allow us to introduce a fair amount of objectivity into the observation process. The fact remains, however, that checklists are simply not a good means of recording data relative to behaviors which occur spontaneously and unpredictably. Rather, a checklist is more appropriate for situations in which certain behaviors, stated in list form, are anticipated (see Chapter Four) and their occurrence verified.

Preparing Records

The preparation and use of all types of records for observation involve similar considerations. Let's deal with these briefly. First of all, we must accept the fact that a certain amount of time and effort is required to develop and use such records. Generally speaking, if a record is relatively easy to devise, we often end up spending a considerable amount of time actually gathering information and interpreting it. On the other hand, some records are fairly difficult to devise, and yet their actual use, and the summary and interpretation of the data gathered, is relatively easy. It seems as if time gained with an easily devised record is lost in its use and interpretation and, vice versa, time and effort spent in extra development is often gained in its more efficient use and interpretation. In the long run, we will spend about the same amount of time on all of the records—if it's not time spent in development, then it will be spent in use and interpretation.

Throughout the development of record forms for observation, the ultimate goal should be a record that allows us to gather information objectively. The designer of record forms might continually ask himself: will there be a high agreement or correlation of the results of various observers who use the record independently? Another way to increase the form's objectivity, and therefore its usability, would be to conduct field tests with the record forms and make pertinent revisions *before* extensive use is made of them. In other words, the forms would be tried out, in pilot study fashion, on a small sample group of children; then revisions would be made depending upon such factors as the ease with which observers were able to use it, problems that observers may have experienced with it, or perhaps a lack of agreement/correlation of the information obtained.

Another consideration related to the preparation and use of all types of records, important enough to inject at this point, is that there must be ample opportunity to observe the behaviors or events of interest contained in a well designed form—or there is no point in having a record form at all!

Operational Definitions

One important element of the record form will be a description of what constitutes an *occurrence* of the behaviors or events of interest. While it is true that observations may sometimes be made in informal *situations,* the observation process *itself* cannot be casual if it is to yield information which will be helpful in making instructional decisions—the behaviors and events being recorded must be specific, accurate, defined. The reason for an accurate description of what constitutes an occurrence of a behavior or event is to add precision to the observation. What constitutes an instance of a behavior or event for Johnny should also constitute an instance for Mary and Peter and Michael and Helen and all of the other children for whom the behavior will be assessed. We cannot change our minds regarding what constitutes an occurrence of the behavior from one time to another and still expect consistency and precision in assessment. Inevitably, lack of precision in information gathering will result in lack of precision in interpretation and instructional decision making.

The behavior or event being recorded should be described so specifically that any time *any* child displays the behavior, it can easily be determined whether or not the behavior has occurred. Some behaviors may prove difficult to describe and, in these instances, a variety of examples which describe instances of the behavior can be given to further specify the descriptions.

Be Specific

We will now consider several examples in the areas of gross motor development and social-emotional development to illustrate possible levels of precision which occur with varying degrees of specificity for operational definitions of the same behavior. Consider what a difference it would make in your observation if the behavior *jumping* was defined on a checklist as:

	Yes	No
The child jumps.	____	____

   or:

	Yes	No
The child jumps forward a distance of at least one foot, from a standing position, and lands on both feet without falling over.	____	____

Think about the possible differences in an observation situation between these two behavior descriptions:

	Yes	No
The child likes school.	_____	_____

or:

	Yes	No
The child makes verbal statements about his liking school without being prompted.	_____	_____

Or what would happen in an observation with this behavior statement:

	Yes	No
The child shares.	_____	_____

as compared with this
behavior description:

If the child is playing with a toy and another child approaches and asks to use the toy, the child gives the toy to the other child without any negative verbal statements.	_____	_____

In each of these examples, the first statement in the pair of behavior descriptions represents an imprecise description and the second statement illustrates a more precise way of describing the behavior.

A considerable amount of time may pass before information which is recorded is collated and used for instructional decision making. Even though an observer may have had it clear in his mind about what was meant by "sharing" at the time the observation was conducted, it is unlikely that he would be able to recall the meaning of "sharing" at the later date when the interpretation is being made. For this reason and for many other reasons, it is essential that a precise description of the behavior or event be a part of the development of record forms for use in the observation process.

Base Decisions on Evidence

Let's suppose a team of teachers are responsible for a group of intermediate level children. Several of the teachers come into contact with situations in which children display oral reading skills because of the pervasive nature of reading in school situations. When asked to make recommendations for a new sequence of objectives in the oral reading program for a child, one teacher said that he thought the new objectives were okay for the child. When asked how he knew this to be so, he said, "Oh, I've heard her read several times and she doesn't have any trouble." Another member of the teaching team, in considering the same decision for the child, suggested that the new objectives might not be appropriate since, "I've been keeping a very careful record of her oral reading behavior in an American literature project she's been independently pursuing and I've collected some evidence that she's having difficulty using punctuation marks as an aid in inflection. Here—do you want to see my record?"

The example is obviously overdone, but it helps to make the point—the second teacher is making a better decision because the evidence exists upon which to base a decision. The first teacher is going about the making of the decision in a very unsystematic way, since evidence about the child's oral reading—if collected at all—is not being brought to bear on the decision to be made.

Be Systematic

The observation record form provides a means of insuring that the same kinds of information are always collected in the observation situation. Unguided, unrecorded, and casual observation is haphazard and meaningless. The record form aids the teacher by forcing him to be objective in his observations. This in turn insures that the information collected using a record form will be definitive and specific, that it will yield meaningful, useful information upon which instructional decisions can be based or questions can be answered. In order to avoid the haphazard approach to observation—not to mention the misapplication of results—it is advisable to experiment with several different ways of recording, describing, or coding behaviors in order to reach that method and format which is the most effective and efficient for a given teacher. A field testing phase in the development process is essential. Revisions should be made before the final forms are developed and made ready for use with learners in classroom situations. Seldom are our first efforts the best, and most people will find that revisions in observation records will do no less than refine, and make more reliable, any judgments and instructional decisions based on them.

Although it is the observer's responsibility to revise an observational record form he has devised, it is also highly desirable to elicit the cooperation of other observers. In this way it is possible to have other observers independently record observations to see if the form reveals substantial agreement among the observers. If the behavior descriptions are precise, there is a much better chance that observers will agree about what they have seen than there is if the behavior descriptions are general and vague.

In summary, the objectivity of the information gained through the observation process can be increased by:

1. Using precise descriptions of the behaviors or events
2. Experimenting with the record form
3. Practicing using the form
4. Having some other observers independently record their observations to check on agreement among observers

PROBLEMS IN RECORD KEEPING

Observation done without record keeping is futile. It is simply not possible for an ordinary human to keep the information he has observed in his head over a period of time and to recall it at a later date. Our memories are unreliable. But simply because we choose to use some kind of record keeping to note the information as it occurs during an observation does not mean that we have solved all of our problems. One of the things that can happen is that inaccuracies can occur—some unexpected behavior might go by unobserved—during the actual recording.

Problems in record keeping

Suppose that a primary level teacher was interested in a child's oral reading behavior. And suppose that this teacher was keeping track of oral reading skills by using a checklist, with two of the possible items from such a checklist shown below. It is possible that the child exhibited the behavior stated in item A of the checklist, but the teacher may have mistakenly checked off item B as being what he observed the child doing. As you can see, any interpretation about the child's ability in oral reading based on such an error would be absolutely incorrect. Here we have an example of a simple clerical error while the record form was being marked. Many other similar inaccuracies can creep into the recording process if attention is not paid to the task at hand.

Oral Reading Checklist

A. Child indicates punctuation by using his
   voice.   Yes _____   No _____

B. Child hesitates when pronouncing most
   words.   Yes __✓__   No _____

As we have said, undertaking observation without using some record keeping device is futile. And, while the use of records does provide an *opportunity* to make and record systematic observations, the use of records does not automatically *guarantee* that the observation will actually be made systematically and objectively. If, for example, subjective interpretations are being made by the observer as he records the information, the objectivity of the final record will be questionable. Interestingly enough, one of the ways to improve the systematic manner in which a person makes his observations is to have someone observe *him* as he observes children. In this way, there is a chance to provide him with an objective record of his own behavior, and he can then analyze the record to determine if he behaves systematically when he observes children.

COLLECTING INFORMATION

Once the purpose for observing has been determined and the observation record has been selected and developed, the actual observation—the collecting of the information—occurs next. Since memory is unreliable, it is most desirable to record the observation as the behavior or event under study is actually occurring. If it is not possible to make the record during the observation (such as, when an individual being observed performs an unexpected behavior during a group discussion or similar participation activity) then the record should be completed as soon as possible following the actual performance of the behavior or occurrence of the event. Usually, however, the process will be such that one child or one event will be observed at a time.

Be Unobtrusive

If teachers strive to make observation a routine, integral part of teaching, then learners will not view their being observed as an extraordinary occurrence and the observation will be unobtrusive. To the extent that we are able to observe unobtrusively, we are more likely to get information about typical behaviors of children. At times it may be necessary to arrange or contrive some special situations in order to insure that a particular behavior of interest will be displayed. However, to the greatest possible extent, if children are unaware that they are being observed, they tend to perform in more natural, typical ways. It might also be said that being unobtrusive and avoiding the contrived situation will enhance the integrity and objectivity of the observation and, probably, the reliability of the data recorded.

Get Lots of Data

As a general rule, the longer the time period available for observation, the more reliable the information obtained is likely to be. A longer time period allows for more opportunities for instances of the behavior to occur. A long time period—preferably a time span encompassing regular intervals during the day and the

various days of the week during the year—provides an opportunity for systematically gathering information covering a variety of situations and behaviors. Furthermore, being able to eliminate the "unusual" situation and "extremes" of behavior tends to yield a more comprehensive and accurate picture of the learner's behavior.

Here Are Some Examples

The checklists on pages 58 and 59 were developed by a teacher who wanted to assess gross motor skills of children in the primary grades. The checklist below shows its application to one child during *one* recess period. The list on page 59 is the same checklist after it had been used for the same child over a period of ten different recess periods.

What can you conclude about the child's gross motor abilities based on the information generated through one day's use of the checklist? Not much. Consider,

Gross Motor Skills Checklist

One Observation

Name: *Sue Slipe*

Observer: *G. P. Cart*

Directions: Indicate if behavior was observed by placing date of occurrence in the blank.

_____	1. Throws ball overhand
10/6	2. Throws ball underhand
_____	3. Catches ball, two hands against body
_____	4. Hops on one foot at least five times
10/6	5. Jumps up and down in place without losing balance
_____	6. Walks balance beam
_____	7. Walks forward heel-to-toe
_____	8. Walks backward heel-to-toe
_____	9. Broad jumps at least one foot from standing position
_____	10. Skips at least fifteen feet without losing rhythm

Name: _____ *Sue Slipe* _____

Observer: _____ *G. P. Cart* _____

Directions: Indicate if behavior was observed by placing date of
occurrence in the blank.

_10/16_   1. Throws ball overhand

_10/6_   2. Throws ball underhand

_____   3. Catches ball, two hands against body

_10/15_   4. Hops on one foot at least five times

_10/6_   5. Jumps up and down in place without losing balance

_10/15_   6. Walks balance beam

_10/10_   7. Walks forward heel-to-toe

_10/10_   8. Walks backward heel-to-toe

_____   9. Broad jumps at least one foot from standing position

_10/21_   10. Skips at least fifteen feet without losing rhythm

though, the possible conclusions emerging from the data collected over ten different time periods. It should be obvious that conclusions drawn from the latter, the extended observation, would be the more justifiable and reliable.

INTERPRETATION

Once information has been collected using observation procedures, it will have to be interpreted. (Remember that behavioral evidence is collected for the purpose of drawing conclusions and, in turn, instructional decisions are made based on the conclusions.) Information on which interpretations will be based should be gathered over an adequate period of time and in a variety of situations to insure that a reliable sampling of behavior is available prior to drawing any conclusions. A single behavioral incident does not afford opportunities for looking at patterns of behavior and does not constitute enough of a base from which to draw inferences about learners. It is only after making a number of observations over a period of time and in a variety of situations that a pattern begins to emerge. It should be remembered that all conclusions—regardless of the extent of the data base—are tentative and subject to continual revision as new information becomes available. Teachers should periodically review the new information that has become available on learners and consider whether previous conclusions ought to be revised or modified.

It is worth noting that, for some purposes and situations, it may be necessary to make observations of several learners in the same situations for comparison purposes. Very often it will not be possible to determine if behavior is typical unless some feeling for what is "normal" or typical of children of similar ages and backgrounds is available. It is also important to keep in mind that the observation records as well as the conclusions drawn from these records are confidential and—particularly in the case of potentially "negative" conclusions which have yet to be verified—they should be handled with care to insure their confidentiality.

SUMMARIZING INFORMATION

We have mentioned earlier that humans are continually behaving. Hundreds of thousands of behaviors are generated by learners in classroom situations each and every day. The teacher is expected to deal with all of this behavioral information in some systematic way in order to make instructional decisions or meet other needs that we have discussed previously.

When teachers use observation methods, they will certainly not be able to make a record of all of the behaviors that occur for any one child in any given day, but they will be able to record a great deal of information about the children in their care. The large amount of information which is recorded through the use of observation methods is sometimes difficult to summarize; however, it is usually necessary to make summaries and to determine patterns of behavior in order to make instructional decisions for the child. Different methods of summarizing information gathered by using various record-keeping forms can be developed. Some methods of summarizing are suggested in association with various types of observation records and are included in later chapters.

Any records, even excellent records, are of no value unless the information is interpreted. We have made this point and emphasized it both in the first chapter and earlier in this chapter. However, it is of such import that it bears repeating again. Information is not gathered as an end in itself; the information is a means to an end and that end is the making of appropriate instructional decisions about the child or meeting other purposes for observation. An unused file of beautifully kept observation records—not being utilized for instructional decisions—merely takes up space. Indeed, one wonders if a teacher who functions in this way is capable of making appropriate instructional decisions at all!

INCREASING EFFICIENCY

There is simply no getting around the fact that observation is a time-consuming process. While some of the record forms for observation enable us to make observations rather efficiently, we still must spend the time developing the record form. So, sooner or later, whether it be in the actual observation or the development of the record or both, we will find ourselves spending a considerable amount of time in observation. It is imperative that we increase the efficiency of observation. The following are some ideas which are likely to result in an increased efficiency of observation.

As a general rule, teachers should become habituated to capitalizing on any and all opportunities to observe. They may be able to make use of the time when learners are working independently. The trend toward types of programs in which learners can function independently appears to be growing, so it is possible that

teachers will have increasingly greater amounts of time available for observation. It is also possible to make use of the time when learners are being supervised by others, such as special teachers, playground supervisors, and older learners tutoring younger learners, to make observations. In other words, teachers should utilize, as much as they can, the times when they are freed from direct responsibilities with learners and should capitalize on this new time for making observations.

It is important to set up some sort of schedule so that certain children are observed every day and so that no children are neglected over the long run. It is also necessary to vary the time periods so that the sample of behavioral evidence resulting from observation is not slanted toward a particular time of the day. It would be incorrect, for example, to always collect observation information shortly before lunch, when children are apt to be hungry and restless—to use any time period consistently, while excluding all other times, would be inappropriate. The individual who is new to the use of observation processes should take comfort in the fact that practice tends to increase efficiency. In general, the more you use observation methods, the more efficient you become, both in their use and in *your* use of time.

Aids Are Available

Another means of increasing the efficiency of observation is to make use of a variety of aids which are available and which tend to increase the accuracy of the observation records. Index cards, small notebooks, or copies of various record forms for different types of observations can be "stashed" at various places throughout the classroom so that time is not spent going to a central file or to the teacher's desk to obtain paper or record forms when the opportunity arises to make an observation. When notebooks, cards, record forms, and even portable tape recorders, are placed in various locations throughout the classroom, they will be handy whenever a record needs to be made. The observer should consider supplementing the observation record with samples of work, drawings, or whatever else may be related to the purpose for which the observation is being made.

A variety of inexpensive counters and timers are available for those situations in which frequencies of behaviors are being tallied or in which time sampling is being used. These consist of items such as a golfer's wrist counter, a kitchen timer, a device to keep track of the amount of purchases in the supermarket, parking meter timer reminders, and many others. It is possible to devise simple shorthand or coding systems so that large amounts of information can be recorded rapidly. We are not suggesting, of course, that teachers learn shorthand as a way of increasing the efficiency of the observation process. However, all of us who have been involved in note-taking situations have worked out some rapid way of recording information using our own personal brand of shorthand or coding schemes. These same kinds of personal shorthand coding can be brought to bear in increasing the efficiency of the observation process.

Finally, although not available to all and constituting items which are more technical than the other aids mentioned, film, still photographs, and even videotape should not be dismissed by the observer who desires added efficiency in the observation process. Films, still photographs and videotape can be used for training teachers in observation procedures as well as for actual observations. Of course, in those instances in which teachers are interested in observing their own behavior, it will be essential to use such aids. There is simply no other way to directly observe one's own behavior.

PROBLEMS ASSOCIATED
WITH THE OBSERVATION PROCESS

There is always the possibility of error in the observation process. In the information evaluation phase, for example, there is simply no way to avoid a certain amount of subjectivity, a factor in the information-gathering procedures as well. One textbook listing of the problems associated with observation procedures indicates that they are inefficient, subjective, unreliable, difficult to interpret, and uneconomical in the use of teacher time. It may be true that many aspects of the observation process involve elements of error. But it is also true that, for many purposes, observation methods represent the *only* way of gathering the necessary information about learners and events. Whereas complete and absolute objectivity is impossible, many controls can be exercised so that the observation which does occur and the data which are recorded are more exact. In other words, refinements are available which tend to diminish the causes of error and increase the reliability of observation.

If observation is not recorded when the behavior occurs, the record may be inaccurate because of a lack of memory of the details on the part of the observer. The means of handling this problem is fairly straightforward—when at all possible, make the record while the observation is being conducted. If control is not exercised, a nonrepresentative sample of behavior may be obtained. If the same time period or the same situations are always used for observation, then a nonrepresentative sample will be obtained. Again, the remedy involves the observer's monitoring his own behavior so that a variety of times and situations are used in gathering observations and a more reliable sample of behavior is likely to be obtained. Care must be exercised so that all learners are observed equally and often—even though, for certain problems, it may be necessary to concentrate on certain "problem" learners and exclude certain others.

And Now for Some Examples

Let's assume that a preschool teacher had been using a checklist to assess children's progress in achieving some objectives in visual and auditory discrimination. Over a period of several weeks the checklists were marked as the various behaviors occurred. When reviewing the information gathered to date, the teacher was

Visual and Auditory Discrimination Checklist

Name: _John S._

Observer: _G. Ellis_

Directions: Indicate if behavior was observed by placing date of occurrence in the blank.

_1/7_	1. Given an object, finds a match from an array of objects
_2/4_	2. Given an object, finds a picture representing the object
_____	3. Points to missing parts of common objects
_1/15_	4. Shown two pictures, tells if they are same or different
_1/18_	5. Says two words with same beginning sounds
_2/16_	6. Given a picture, locates a match from an array of pictures
_____	7. Recognizes common sounds when listening to a tape recording
_3/26_	8. Tells if sounds match when presented with pairs of sounds
_3/3_	9. Finds two matching sound boxes from an array of sound boxes
_3/19_	10. Tells if two words rhyme when he listens to teacher say pairs of words

especially interested in the completed checklists for two children, John and Eric, reproduced on pages 64 and 65. Note the dates on which observations were made for the two boys. Since the times Eric was observed appear to be less frequent than those occasions on which John was observed, it is difficult to make a realistic interpretation. We don't know if Eric ever performed the behaviors after the first time the checklist was used or if the teacher simply neglected to mark his checklist as he displayed the behaviors over a longer period of time. It appears that a more comprehensive set of data exists about John's auditory and visual discrimination abilities than exists for Eric.

Visual and Auditory Discrimination Checklist

Name: _____ *Eric* _____

Observer: _____ *G. Ellis* _____

Directions: Indicate if behavior was observed by placing date of occurrence in the blank.

_____ 1. Given an object, finds a match from an array of objects

_2/26_ 2. Given an object, finds a picture representing the object

_____ 3. Points to missing parts of common objects

_____ 4. Shown two pictures, tells if they are same or different

_____ 5. Says two words with same beginning sounds

_____ 6. Given a picture, locates a match from an array of pictures

_____ 7. Recognizes common sounds when listening to a tape recording

_____ 8. Tells if sounds match when presented with pairs of sounds

_1/7_ 9. Finds two matching sound boxes from an array of sound boxes

_____ 10. Tells if two words rhyme when he listens to teacher say pairs of words

Here's a slightly different type of example which illustrates one of the other problems associated with observation: On Monday, Sara did the following things in gym period:

1. turned forward somersault
2. turned cartwheel
3. did handstand
4. did back flip
5. jumped on trampoline

On Friday, the teacher was making records of the weekly accomplishments and he completed a record for Sara as follows:

Date: _____9/13_____

Name: _____*Sara Jason*_____

Sara was able to do a back flip for the first time this week. _____

Notice the discrepancy between Sara's actual behaviors and the teacher's record of the behaviors as a result of several days elapsing between the actual display of the behaviors (the opportunity for observation) and the completion of the record form.

To illustrate how limited contact can cause misinterpretation even when records are accurate, consider the case of the itinerant art teacher. Over a period of weeks she produced a set of anecdotal records for Ginny. She concluded that Ginny was a model student—well behaved and pleasant with adults and other children. It turns out, though, that Ginny loves art and little else. The rest of her school day is spent getting into and out of trouble with peers and teachers alike. You can see that when Ginny's art teacher drew some conclusions about her social-emotional development on the basis of the anecdotes, she was badly mistaken. The inaccurate inference made by the art teacher was at least partly due to the nonrepresentativeness of the sample of Ginny's behavior, based as it was on the same activity, at the same time each day—thus, the art teacher's inference was biased. The diversity of Ginny's behavior throughout the school day did not show itself on this teacher's records, a poor representation of Ginny's social-emotional behavioral repertoire.

Observer's Biases

There are certain known tendencies and biases which reside in the observer and which can present problems when using observation methods. Certain of these tendencies and biases are more likely to occur in association with some observation records than with others. Let's consider these biases and the associated record forms now.

There is a tendency to give a higher or lower rating to a behavior than it really deserves when a generally favorable or unfavorable impression is made on the observer by the behavior or, for that matter, by the child. This tendency—to give a higher rating than ought to be given because of a generally favorable attitude toward the learner—could be called the *halo effect.* This error occurs mostly in the use of rating scales, in which a degree of judgment is involved. It must be remembered that, when recording behaviors on a rating scale, the observer should attempt to make only a record of the behavior that occurred and not evaluate. If the rater can keep this in mind, he may be able to monitor his rating of behavior so that he is more realistic. A similar type of error can occur in using anecdotal records, in which the observer might tend to record only positive instances of behavior for those learners toward whom he has a generally favorable attitude and note more negative instances of behavior for those children toward whom he holds a generally unfavorable attitude.

One way to improve on the reliability of such ratings is to use several ratings taken by a number of different observers at the same time. Although not a practical solution in those school situations in which a teacher generally works with one group of children and does not have other adults who might serve as co-observers, this approach would increase the objectivity of the process.

A Pause for an Example

For some teachers, the halo effect might occur because of the type of dress and the cleanliness of learners. Those children who are generally clean and well dressed tend to create positive feelings between themselves and the teacher and, even if these same children misbehave, the teacher is likely to discount their behavior as a "once in a lifetime" occurrence rather than typical behavior. Similarly, those children who are generally unclean and unkempt may create an aura of negative feeling between themselves and the teacher; and, consequently, these children may receive low or negative ratings on behaviors even though they may really be "at the head of the class."

Many similar examples could be cited. Children who are somewhat divergent in their thinking may not be given credit for the creativity they exhibit if the teacher is the type who is expecting the child to give only a certain answer to a problem. Also we can all think back to our own school experiences and probably quickly call to mind the situation in which some child was "teacher's pet," meaning, of course, the halo effect was operating and that child was so well thought of by the teacher that he could do no wrong—no matter if the rest of us *knew* how many wrongs he really performed!

Is Objectivity Possible?

It has been pointed out that absolute objectivity is impossible in any information-gathering procedure and that observation methods in general involve more subjective judgment than some other evaluation procedures. This is particularly true when rating scales are used as the record-keeping form for an observation. The nature of the rating scale is such that more evaluative judgments are called for by the observer than in such other records as checklists, participation charts, and anecdotal records. It has also been mentioned that, even though there may be error associated with the observation process, teachers often have no other alternative than to use observation methods. Of course, teachers can make a different kind of an error, too, in that they sometimes use observation when another assessment procedure, such as a test would be more appropriate. No data gathering procedure is completely free of error or devoid of problems. Observation should not be deleted as a data-gathering method because it has associated problems, but its limitations should be known to the user so that attention can be given to reducing possible errors.

One of the major difficulties of using observation for information-gathering purposes is that it is a time-consuming process. When one considers the time involved in the development of some other intricate information-gathering procedures, however, the time required for using observation is put into proper prospective, and we discover that observation may not be as time consuming as it appears to be on the surface.

Other Errors

Another common error is that of rating *all* learners too high, too low, or average on a characteristic. When all learners are rated too high, we call it a "generosity error," and when learners are rated too low, we call it a "severity error." (It is interesting to note that the generosity error occurs somewhat more often than the severity error.) In the generosity error situation, the rater tends to favor the high end of the scale for all the learners he is observing, and in the severity error, he tends to favor the lower end of the scale. It is also possible to err in rating all learners near the center of the scale. This problem is generally referred to as the "central tendency error." The result of this error is that everyone tends to be rated as average and no rating differences accrue to indicate actual differences that exist among learners.

The generosity error, the severity error, and the central tendency error occur most often in relation to the use of rating scales, but they can also occur in a slightly different form with the use of anecdotal records. When making anecdotal records, there seems to be a general tendency on the part of teachers to record disrupting behaviors more often than normal behaviors. This is a pattern which has been discerned from reviewing numerous anecdotal records. Unless a teacher is aware of this tendency and consistently monitors his behavior so that it does not occur, we are likely to find more disrupting behaviors recorded on anecdotal records than typical or normal behaviors.

The fact that the observer himself approves or disapproves of the behavior he is observing may influence the observation. This problem can apply to all kinds of record forms. If the error does not creep in as the observation is actually being made, as it would in an anecdotal record, it may creep in when the record form is being developed, as in the checklist. There may, for example, be an imbalance in the behaviors included in the checklist because of the developer's biases.

Another error ought to be mentioned at this point. If two characteristics are rated about the same because the observer incorrectly assumes there is a relationship between the characteristics, the problem is referred to as a "logical error." When a teacher makes such an assumption about two characteristics, and if he is already aware of the pupil's standing or rating on one characteristic, he is likely to rate the child the same way on the second characteristic. In an example of "logical error," if a child has a history of excelling in sports activities, the teacher might be likely to rate him higher than he deserves on other motor activities, revealing the teacher's belief—even though it may not be correct—that sports and motor activities are always synonymous. In this instance, the observer or rater has some preconceived ideas about the relationships between characteristics, and he does not consider the effect that his ideas about these relationships might have on the observations and resulting decisions regarding the learner.

Consider, for example, the plight of this special educator, and also consider the probably poor instructional decisions that might evolve out of an assumption. Suppose this teacher thinks—indeed, is convinced—that there is a one-to-one relationship between speech production and language development and makes instructional decisions based on this belief. The special educator is responsible for a group of seven learners who exhibit a variety of learning problems. For example, articulation is difficult for many of the children—they have motor problems which cause their speech to be somewhat unintelligible. The teacher is aware of these articulation problems, has even recorded information about them, and has also concluded that these same children are lagging in language development. In point of fact, the children are every bit as well off in language development as other children of the same age. An inappropriate inference was drawn because the teacher thought there was a one-to-one relationship between speech and language—while the real causes, probably varying for each of the seven children, passed by unnoticed.

Several other similar biases reside within the observer and can limit the usability of information gathered through observation. If the observer happens to be in a bad mood, the observation may not be objective. It has been found that biases can indirectly result from such variables as the observer's age, sex, his own need for approval, and many other factors.

CONTROLLING ERROR

Even though sources of bias can never be completely eliminated, they can be controlled. We have mentioned earlier that it is impossible to make observation an error-free process since it is conducted by humans, and it is only human to be subjective to some extent about what we do. We must, however, take precautions to make our assessment procedures as precise and error-free as possible. If the observer is aware that certain biases are likely to influence his observation, he can consciously monitor his behavior to try to eliminate them. Many observers are not aware of the general tendencies and biases which reside in observers (the halo effect, the generosity error, the logical error), but if they are informed of the possible sources of error they can exercise some control over their biases.

It is possible to limit the amount of error in the observation process through training and practice in the methods. While training in observation and record-keeping processes can reduce errors, we must remember that these errors cannot be entirely eradicated. Our interpretations of information gathered using observation methods, then, should be tentative. All conclusions that we reach about learners need to be checked continually and corroborated through further information gathered through both observation and other assessment methods.

Check for Objectivity

An excellent procedure for reducing the error involved in observation is to arrange a situation in which several individuals can observe the learners or the events independently, make their records independently, and then pool their information. As a means of looking carefully at the objectivity of their observations, teachers may even work out a system where they can serve as "checkers" for each other. It is particularly helpful to have someone come in from outside the classroom to check the teacher's observations, since it is much more likely that the teacher who is involved with the learners day after day will exhibit the biases we have been discussing; this "outsider" should not know the learners as well. Independent observers may even be able to help teachers revise their record-keeping forms for observation methods. Teachers may have missed listing significant behavior that another observer might suggest be added to the record form.

It is also possible that the observer has attempted to obtain information about too many behaviors simultaneously. This is particularly true of individuals new to the observation method. In the beginning especially, only a few behaviors should be chosen, and the record-keeping and observation process related to these behaviors should be revised and operating smoothly before the beginning observer attempts to deal with many behaviors.

One other difficulty involved with the use of observation methods is that there is a considerable amount of information gathered about the learners. Often it is difficult to process and summarize varieties of information so that meaningful interpretations about it can be made. One possible way of dealing with this problem is to become more selective in observations, to focus on behaviors which tend to be representative of a host of behaviors. For example, it may be possible to use shorter periods of time in a time-sampling procedure as one becomes more proficient in the use of the technique. The ability to become properly selective will grow with practice in observation.

Be Aware of Biases

We have seen, then, that there is ample room for error in the process of observation and that different kinds of error are likely to be associated with different record-keeping procedures. Many aspects of the observation process tend to increase the margin of error involved in gathering information. Observation just happens to be a somewhat more subjective procedure than some other information-gathering procedures; but—and this is a big *but*—observation is often the only reasonable information-gathering procedure to use for many purposes. There are certain inherent tendencies and biases in observers which influence and introduce error into the observation process. Even though these sources of bias can never be completely eliminated, they can be controlled. This is especially possible if the observer is aware of these biases and can then consciously monitor his behavior in an attempt to reduce or eliminate them.

SUMMARY

This chapter included information about the general methods of making an observation and the considerations involved in developing and using record forms for observations. A discussion of the problems typically associated with the use of observation methods was also presented.

The observation process consists of these basic steps: First, the purpose for making the observation must be determined since all other decisions and steps in the observation process are dependent upon the purpose. Next, the type of record form to be used in the observation must be determined and the form must be developed. Third, the actual observation or series of observations must be conducted. And, finally, interpretations that fulfill the purposes for the observations must be made. Throughout the entire process, the observer must take care to see that all possible error is eliminated from the observation, forms development, record keeping, and interpretation.

Means of increasing the efficiency of observation were presented. Also, problems associated with the use of observation as an assessment procedure were discussed, and possible solutions were presented. It was noted that many aspects of the observation process tend to increase the error involved in data gathering. Also, those known tendencies and biases which reside in observers and which influence the objectivity of the observations were discussed. Even though sources of bias can never be completely eliminated, it was indicated that there are ways of controlling subjectivity and reducing the margin of error involved in gathering information.

ACTIVITY 1

Here's a way to refine your ability to devise operational definitions of teacher behaviors.

1. Choose an area of teacher behavior which is of interest to you and prepare an operational definition of the behavior.
2. Choose appropriate places and times, and conduct the observation by tallying the number of times the behavior occurs.
3. After you've conducted this observation several times, decide if your operational definition of the behavior is adequate. If necessary, revise the definition and repeat the observation.

ACTIVITY 2

Here's an activity which may help you to be more precise and objective in observation. You and a colleague will work as a team on this activity. Here's how to proceed:

1. Choose a child to observe. As they observe the child, both observers should use Checklist A, on pages 75 and 77.

2. Choose a different child for this observation. Both observers should use Checklist B on pages 79 and 81 as they observe this child.

3. After completing both checklists, compare your results. How closely did you and your colleague agree? Which checklist resulted in closer agreement, form A or form B?

Checklist A

Date:_____

*Name:*_____

*Observer:*_____

Directions: Place a checkmark in the column labeled *Yes* if the behavior was observed. Mark the *No* column if the behavior was not observed.

	Yes	No
1. Child likes reading	____	____
2. Child pays attention	____	____
3. Child solves problems independently	____	____
4. Child helps other children	____	____
5. Child enjoys outdoor activities	____	____
6. Child is a leader	____	____
7. Child accepts responsibility	____	____
8. Child exercises initiative	____	____

Checklist A

Date:_____

Name:_____

Observer:_____

Directions: Place a checkmark in the column labeled *Yes* if the behavior was observed. Mark the *No* column if the behavior was not observed.

	Yes	No
1. Child likes reading	___	___
2. Child pays attention	___	___
3. Child solves problems independently	___	___
4. Child helps other children	___	___
5. Child enjoys outdoor activities	___	___
6. Child is a leader	___	___
7. Child accepts responsibility	___	___
8. Child exercises initiative	___	___

Checklist B

Date: _____

Name: _____

Observer: _____

Directions: Place a checkmark in the column labeled *Yes* if the behavior was observed. Mark the *No* column if the behavior was not observed.

	Yes	No
1. Child smiles during a reading activity.	____	____
2. Child makes a positive statement about reading such as ''I like reading.''	____	____
3. When given a task, child completes it in the allotted time.	____	____
4. Child demonstrates how to do something for another child.	____	____
5. Child completes a task without seeking help from the teacher or other children.	____	____
6. Other children choose this child to be the leader in an activity.	____	____
7. Child carries out an assigned responsibility without being reminded.	____	____
8. Child makes positive comment about outdoor activity.	____	____

Checklist B

*Name:*_____

*Observer:*_____

Directions: Place a checkmark in the column labeled *Yes* if the behavior was observed. Mark the *No* column if the behavior was not observed.

	Yes	No
1. Child smiles during a reading activity.	_____	_____
2. Child makes a positive statement about reading such as "I like reading."	_____	_____
3. When given a task, child completes it in the allotted time.	_____	_____
4. Child demonstrates how to do something for another child.	_____	_____
5. Child completes a task without seeking help from the teacher or other children.	_____	_____
6. Other children choose this child to be the leader in an activity.	_____	_____
7. Child carries out an assigned responsibility without being reminded.	_____	_____
8. Child makes positive comment about outdoor activity.	_____	_____

THREE

Behavior tallying and charting

One of the easiest ways for the observer to record behaviors as they occur is simply to tally the behavior each time it occurs. This chapter is about the procedures used in tallying (counting) and charting (graphing) observed behaviors.

When you complete this chapter and the recommended activities, you should be able to:

1. Determine if behavior tallying and charting should be used when given descriptions of different observation purposes
2. Count number of times behaviors occur and determine duration of behavior
3. Compute rates of behavior
4. Use time sampling when observing behaviors which occur at very high rates over long periods of time
5. Prepare bar charts or graphs to summarize data on frequency of occurrence of behaviors or the duration of behaviors

FREQUENCY COUNTS AND TIME SAMPLING

For some purposes, the only type of record needed for the observation is a simple count of the frequency of occurrence of a specific behavior. This is particularly true in association with precision teaching and behavior modification efforts. However, the process of tallying behaviors and preparing behavior charts should not be viewed as being limited to precision teaching and behavior modification situations. In fact, information collected by tallying behaviors may be used subsequently to design checklists or rating scales, or as the basis for completing checklists and rating scales.

In some instances, the *duration* of the behavior—such as the amount of time a child spends painting a picture or looking at a book—may be needed. It may be also desirable to compute rates of behavior for some learners and to determine how many times a behavior occurs in a specified amount of time. "Pictures" of the pattern of occurrences of the behavior over a time period can be obtained by preparing a simple bar chart or frequency graph.

Counting Behaviors

One prerequisite for being able to make tallies of behaviors is that the behaviors must be clearly defined in observable terms so that the observer knows when an instance of a behavior has really occurred. You will recall that examples of precise versus vague descriptions of behaviors were included in Chapter Two. The process of continuously recording each behavior or event as it occurs by using tallies is most appropriate for behaviors that are discrete units and that occur fairly infrequently during a day. In other words, it must be possible to describe a unit of behavior so that it is separate and distinct from other behaviors.

Duration of Behavior

There are, of course, some behaviors which are very difficult to describe as discrete units of behaviors. For those types of behaviors which are hard to break into discrete units, the *duration* of a behavior may be recorded. We would be interested here in the length of time a behavior continued to be performed by the child. For example, a behavior such as sitting in a seat is likely to involve a number of verbal and gestural behaviors other than merely sitting in the seat. Since it might be difficult to distinguish these as discrete behaviors, the more appropriate procedure might be simply to record the length of time the child spends sitting in the seat regardless of the other behaviors that may occur while he is sitting there. The duration is, then, the amount of time spent performing the behavior however it may be described.

Of course, it is still important to describe the behavioral event as specifically as possible so that adequate time periods can be recorded. When it is found that the time period, or duration of the behavior, varies considerably from day to day, it is often desirable to total the amounts of time recorded for a specific behavior and then compute an average rate per some specified time period, such as a day, for the behavior. Rate would be determined here by dividing the *total* of the amounts of time of the behavior by the number of days. So, if we had a total of 83 minutes of crying over a five-day period of time, we would divide 83 by 5 to find an average of 16.6 minutes of crying per day.

And Now for Some Examples

Some examples of behaviors that qualify as separate units (the mere occurrence of which could be tallied) are:

1. touches nose
2. kicks ball
3. raises hand
4. interrupts another person
5. reads sentence orally
6. throws beanbag at target
7. sharpens pencil
8. puts book on shelf

Compare the preceding list with these behaviors which are difficult to describe as discrete units:

1. crying
2. walking around the room
3. eating lunch
4. sitting on the floor
5. listening to records
6. looking out the window
7. giggling
8. modeling clay

You would need to record *duration* of these behaviors.

Time Sampling

For behaviors which occur at high rates, an excellent technique of recording observations is time sampling. Time sampling involves the recording of behaviors at certain times rather than continuously. When using time sampling procedures, predetermined time periods—such as ten minutes during the morning and ten minutes during the afternoon or one half hour period daily—might be used. It is then possible to observe these high frequency behaviors during only short periods of time and to make predictions about total behavior on the basis of the sample.

When using time sampling procedures, the observer should be sure to use predetermined time periods within which to observe the behavior. Fluctuations beyond these predetermined times are not encouraged. The length of time to be used in recording the behavior will depend on the specific behavior of interest. It may be possible, for example, to record the number of times a behavior occurs or the duration of behavior during the first five minutes of each hour, or during variable time blocks, several times over the course of a day.

An example of a behavior which might occur at a high rate is "clinging to an adult." Suppose that a certain child displays this behavior almost continuously. Rather than concentrating on continuously observing the clinging behavior, the teacher might decide to use time sampling. Let's say the teacher decides to observe and note duration of the clinging behavior for two 15-minute time periods in the morning and two more 15-minute time periods in the afternoon. The teacher might watch for clinging behavior from 9:00 to 9:15 a.m. and from 10:45 to 11:00 a.m., and then again from 1:15 to 1:30 p.m. and from 2:45 to 3:00 p.m. The decision about *which* and *how many* time periods to use is somewhat arbitrary, but there are some guidelines which can be used. The teacher should make the decision on the basis of previous experiences with the behavior and should be sure that the time periods chosen coincide with a variety of activities.

Whatever the time periods chosen for time sampling, the behavior should be observed during those periods and ignored (not observed and recorded) at other times. If some unexpected incident related to the behavior occurs at some other time, it can be recorded using an anecdotal record.

RECORD FORMS FOR FREQUENCY AND DURATION

For those behaviors which are discrete units and can be tallied or counted, a record form can be prepared so that tally marks are made each time the behavior is observed. Suppose a teacher is concerned about a child hitting other children and wants a record of frequency of his hitting behavior to use when consulting with a resource person about the child. The record form might look like the one for Tom Lipsitt, on page 88.

A similar type of record form should be prepared for observations of the duration of behavior. Suppose a teacher is interested in determining the duration of "wandering around the room" behavior. The teacher has decided to use time sampling and will observe for one-half hour in the morning (9:00-9:30 a.m.) and again for one-half hour in the afternoon (2:00-2:30 p.m.). The record form might look like the one for Carol Parker, page 89.

Date: *from* _____ *April 1* _____ *to* _____ *April 5* _____

Name: _____ *Tom Lipsitt* _____

Observer: _____ *T. Bradley* _____

Description of Behavior: *Hitting—any deliberate physical contact made*
_____ *with the hands to another child* _____

Days	Tallies	Total
1	卌 ///	8
2	卌 卌 //	12
3	卌 ////	9
4	卌 卌 //	12
5	卌 /	6

Average per day = *9.4 hitting behavior per day for the week*

PREPARING BAR CHARTS AND GRAPHS

The information which is obtained either through tallying frequencies of behavior or through recording duration of behavior (either with or without time-sampling procedures) is generally easier to use and interpret if it is transferred to some kind of a graph or chart. Two of the most useful graphs are a simple bar chart or a frequency graph. The latter graphs tend to be easier to prepare and use than bar charts.

Graphs should be clearly labeled to indicate the type of behavior recorded, the time period involved, and any other information needed to interpret the observations. Convention dictates that the horizontal line or axis be the number of observation periods (such as days); and the vertical line or axis be used to represent the behavior being counted or timed. When some kind of teaching procedure has been used, to determine the differences between before and after teaching, it is possible to place observations from different phases on the same graph to facilitate comparison.

Record for Duration of Behavior

Date: from *11/18/73* to *11/22/73*

Name: *Carol Parker*

Observer: *R. Stephens*

Description of Behavior: *Wandering around the room—any aimless movement by child around the room; asked where he's going, he cannot state a purpose.*

Days	Time from – to		Total Minutes
1	9:05 – 9:22		
	9:27 – 9:30		
	2:03 – 2:10		
	2:18 – 2:30		39
2	9:00 – 9:30		
	2:10 – 2:21		
	2:28 – 2:30		43
3	9:20 – 9:30		
	2:05 – 2:10		
	2:14 – 2:21		
	2:25 – 2:30		27
4	9:00 – 9:30		
	2:00 – 2:18		48
5	9:00 – 9:12		
	9:18 – 9:22		
	2:10 – 2:28		34

Average = *38.2 minutes per day*

Examples of Bar Charts and Graphs

Figure 3-1 is a simple bar chart using information gathered earlier for Tom Lipsitt, the number of his "hitting" behaviors over a five-day period. Figure 3-2 is the same information translated to a frequency graph.

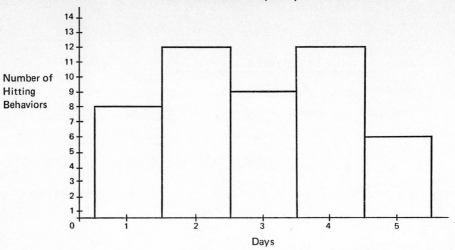

FIGURE 3-1   Tom Lipsitt's "hitting" behavior as observed from April 1 to April 5

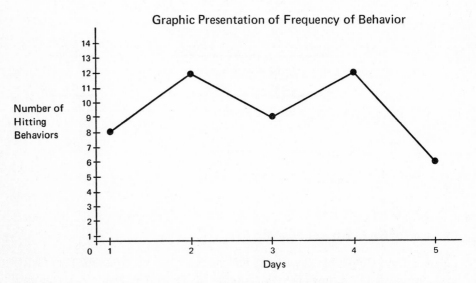

FIGURE 3-2   Tom Lipsitt's "hitting" behavior as observed from April 1 to April 5

Figures 3-3 and 3-4 are graphic representations for Carol Parker's "wandering around the room" behavior, used earlier as an example of a behavior for which duration should be recorded.

Line graphs (Figures 3-2 and 3-4) are easier and faster to prepare than the bar charts. (You can try both types and see which you find easier.) One of the reasons

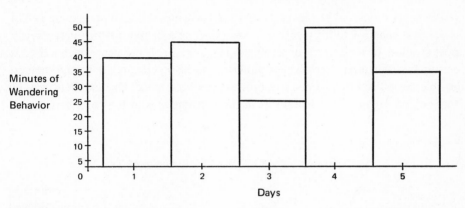

Bar Chart for Duration of Behavior

FIGURE 3-3   Carol Parker's "wandering" behavior as observed from November 18 to November 22

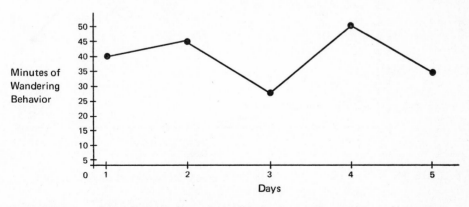

Graphic Presentation of Duration of Behavior

FIGURE 3-4   Carol Parker's "wandering" behavior as observed from November 18 to November 22

we recommend the line graphs is that it is easier to show several behaviors on the same graph when the line type graph is used. For example, let's use our old friend Tom Lipsitt. Suppose we wanted to compare his "hitting" behavior with his "sharing" behavior. After tallying both behaviors, information for both could be transferred to the same graph for ease in comparing, as shown in Figure 3-5.

MODIFYING BEHAVIOR

Teachers are interested in *changing* behaviors—whether this involves helping a child add a new behavior to his repertoire, strengthening a behavior which may already exist at a low or weak level, or eliminating an undesirable behavior which a child is performing. Whatever the behavior modification being effected, it is important to be able to tell whether or not any progress has been made. One excellent way of checking on progress or achievement in these instances is to look at a base rate of

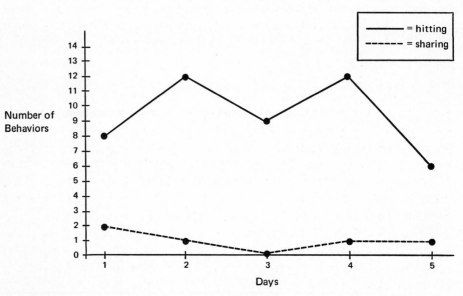

FIGURE 3-5   Tom Lipsitt's "hitting and sharing" behaviors as observed from April 1 to April 5

behavior and then to record the frequency of the behavior after the teaching procedure has been used. By comparing the frequencies or strengths of the behaviors before and after the teaching, it is possible to determine whether or not the specific teaching procedure used has been an effective one.

Base Rates

When we check the frequency of occurrence of behavior over a period of time, we are getting what is called *baseline data* on the behavior. The teacher simply notes the time at the beginning of the observation, counts and tallies each time the specific behavior of interest occurs, and indicates the time at the end of the observation period. A *base rate* can then be calculated by determing the frequency of the behavior per minute or the frequency per half hour or hour, or some other indicated time period. Determining the base rate is a way of identifying a relevant characteristic. The base rate tells us how the child was doing *before* any teaching toward changing that behavior occurred.

Graphic Presentations of Behavior Changes

The procedures for preparing the graph with which we can check for behavior changes over a period of time are the same as those described earlier. We simply divide the horizontal axis into the time periods of interest and proceed as usual.

Here's an Example

Suppose a child named Sam habitually left his possessions lying about the room and continually lost things. He indicated to the teacher that he felt he needed to work on learning to put his things away and she agreed to help him. Together they worked out a plan to count the number of "put-away" behaviors Sam performed before any special teaching procedures were instituted. (They were, in effect, determining his entry behavior.) Remember that this is called baseline data. Check the first section of the graph in Figure 3-6 and you will see that, over a five-day period, Sam's put-away behaviors per hour were minimal. You may wonder why the time is spent taking baseline information. This is done so that there is a basis for comparison to evaluate progress and to assess the effectiveness of the teaching procedures used.

After recording the baseline information on the graph, Sam and his teacher worked out a procedure whereby every time Sam put his things away, he would

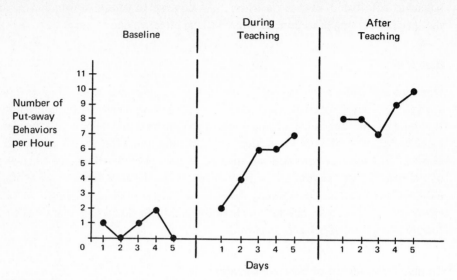

FIGURE 3-6   Changes in Sam Irwin's "put-away" behaviors over a three-week period

receive a token. The tokens could be saved and traded for some special treat later. Check the second section of the graph in Figure 3-6 to see what happened during the next five-day period, the teaching phase. Notice that Sam's put-away behaviors are increasing.

After a period of time, the procedure of using the tokens was altered so that Sam didn't always receive a token. Sometimes he did and sometimes he didn't. We've called this phase "after teaching." During this third phase (also five days), Sam and his teacher again recorded his put-away behaviors. Check the third section of the graph in Figure 3-6 and you will see that Sam is still performing the put-away behaviors at a high level. By comparing the third section of the graph with the first, you can see that Sam has made a lot of progress in the area of putting things away. To both teacher and child the record indicates several items which have a bearing on future instructional decisions. There is now evidence that the method they used for changing behaviors was successful. They have also learned that the child can cooperate in planning and executing the behavior change projects.

Notice that throughout this example, Sam worked closely with his teacher. We deliberately set up this example in this manner so we could make the point that children and teachers can work together on behavior change projects. It is even possible for children to count behaviors and prepare their own records independently.

SUMMARY

This chapter was a presentation of the procedures used in counting, tallying, and graphing observed behaviors. One of the easiest ways to record behaviors as they are being observed is simply to tally the behavior each time it occurs. It is appropriate to obtain frequencies for those behaviors which are discrete units such as ear tugging, spelling a word, or any other similar behaviors. Some behaviors are difficult to describe as discrete units of behavior and, for these behaviors, the duration of the behavior will be recorded. Duration is simply the amount of time spent performing the behavior. In each case, the behavior must be operationally defined so that observers are in agreement as to what constitutes an occurrence of the behavior. When behaviors occur at very high rates, time-sampling procedures can be used instead of recording the behaviors continuously.

It was noted that information about frequency of behavior or duration of behavior is usually easier to interpret if it is transferred to a graph or chart. Line graphs were recommended over the bar chart. Procedures for presenting information about several behaviors simultaneously were presented, as were procedures for recording information about behavior changes over a period of time.

ACTIVITY 1

Here's an opportunity to check your skills of counting behaviors and preparing a graph for the behaviors.

1. Choose a child who exhibits some behavior of interest to you.
2. Be sure the behavior is one which is a discrete unit and can be counted. Prepare an operational definition of the behavior.
3. Observe and tally the occurrences of the behavior for five days, using the record form we've provided on page 97.
4. Translate your tallies to a graph, following the procedures described in this chapter.

ACTIVITY 2

Here's an opportunity to check your skills of noting duration of behaviors and preparing a graph for the behaviors.

1. Choose a child who exhibits some behavior of interest to you.

2. Be sure the behavior is one which is occurring at a high rate and is not a discrete unit so that it is a candidate for observing duration rather than frequency. Prepare an operational definition of the behavior.

3. Use time sampling and make a decision about the time periods to be used for the observations.

4. Observe and note duration of the behavior during the time periods chosen for five days. Use the record form we've provided (page 99) to record your observations.

5. Translate your data to a graph following the procedures described in this chapter.

Record for Frequency of Behavior

Date: *from* _____ *to* _____

Name: _____

Observer: _____

Description of Behavior: _____

_____

Days	Tallies	Total
1	_____	_____
2	_____	_____
3	_____	_____
4	_____	_____
5	_____	_____

Average per day = _____

Record for Duration of Behavior

Date: from_____ to_____

Name: _____

*Observer:*_____

Description of Behavior: _____

_____

Days	Time		Total Minutes
	from	*to*	
	_____		_____
	_____		_____
	_____		_____
	_____		_____
	_____		_____
	_____		_____

Average =

FOUR

Checklists, participation charts, and rating scales

Three types of record forms used in observation are checklists, participation charts, and rating scales. This chapter is a description of these record forms, with suggestions for their development and use. These forms can also be used for other purposes, such as evaluation of learners' written products, but those uses are beyond the scope of this book.

When you complete this chapter and the recommended activities, you should be able to:

1. Determine whether to use a checklist, participation chart, or rating scale when given a variety of observation situations
2. Develop and use checklists for observations
3. Develop and use participation charts for observations
4. Develop and use rating scales for observations
5. Revise checklists, participation charts, and rating scales on the basis of field test experiences

CHECKLISTS

Checklists provide an efficient means of recording the presence or absence of specific behaviors in given situations. The checklist consists of a list of statements about behaviors which are expected to be exhibited. For each statement on the list, there is a place to indicate whether or not the behavior was observed. Therefore, checklists call for simple yes-no determinations on the part of the observer. Basically, checklists provide a means of recording whether a behavior is present or not, or more specifically, whether the behavior was observed or not at the time the checklist was used. Usually a check mark, or other indicator, is placed in the appropriate space on the checklist form (see, for example, the Mathematics Checklist on page 103 if the observation indicates the presence of the behavior.

Notice in the Mathematics Checklist that, for items 3, 5, and 6 the child's behavior must coincide with *all* parts of the item before a mark is made to indicate he exhibited the behavior. If the teacher expects the child will be able to perform some but not all of the item, the items containing more than one part could be revised to describe a single behavior. For example, the current item 6 could become three items: _____points to penny, _____ points to nickel, _____points to dime.

Many other behaviors important in math are not included on this checklist. That is because these other behaviors are of the type in which the child makes his own written record. Of course, many more items would be needed for a complete assessment of math skills and understandings at the primary level.

Often the checklist is set up so that the *absence* of a mark indicates the

behavior was *not* observed. In other types of checklist formats, there are spaces to indicate both presence and absence (for instance, see the Fine Motor Skills Checklist, page 104), and a mark is always made in the appropriate column as per the information generated during the observation.

Appropriate Use of Checklists

Checklists should be used when the behaviors to be exhibited are known in advance and when there is no need to provide an indication of the frequency and/or quality characteristics of the performance. If frequency or quality characteristics are needed, then a different kind of record will be required for the observation. As you will see later, when there is no possibility of discerning the behaviors in advance, it

Mathematics Checklist

Primary Level

Date: _____

Name: _____

Observer: _____

Directions: Place a checkmark next to the item if the behavior was observed. Leave the space blank if the behavior was *not* observed.

_____ 1. Counts to 10 without error

_____ 2. Points to an empty set

_____ 3. Puts objects into sets of 1 to 5

_____ 4. Places objects in one-to-one correspondence

_____ 5. Finds paper cutouts of geometric objects: circle, square, triangle, and rectangle

_____ 6. Points to pennies, nickels, and dimes

_____ 7. Counts to 50 by 2s

_____ 8. Finds a one cup measure

_____ 9. Walks on the number line as directed

_____ 10. Compares objects and shows which is bigger and smaller

Fine Motor Skills Checklist

Date:_____

Name:_____

Observer:_____

Directions: Place an X in the **Yes** column if the behavior is observed;
place an X in the **No** column if the behavior is not
observed.

	Yes	No
1. Touches forefingers together on first trial	____	____
2. Makes a stack of two small blocks	____	____
3. Makes a stack of four small blocks	____	____
4. Makes a stack of eight small blocks	____	____
5. Dumps object out of small container without dropping container	____	____
6. Holds pencil to make a mark on paper	____	____
7. Uses pincer grasp to pick up small object	____	____
8. Passes small object from one hand to the other without dropping object	____	____

will be necessary to use an anecdotal record. But for those situations in which the behaviors to be displayed by the learners are anticipated or able to be anticipated in advance, and when there is a need to simply provide information about the presence or absence of the behavior, then the checklist provides the most useful and objective record-keeping device for that situation.

Advantages of Checklists

One of the advantages of using a checklist is that a great deal of behavioral information can be recorded very rapidly (see the Materials Available Checklist on page 105). This is partially due to the preplanning that has gone into the development of the checklist. The efficiency of using a checklist can be facilitated by arranging the statements on the checklist in certain ways. For example, the listing

Materials Available Checklist

Materials which are likely to be found in early childhood education programs are listed below in alphabetical order. If the classroom includes these materials *so that children have free access to them,* place a checkmark in the box. If the classroom does not include the materials or if it does have the materials but the children do not have free access to the materials, do not put a checkmark in the box.

School: _____ Date:_____

Teacher: _____ Observer: _____

☐ Balance beam	☐ Housekeeping center—equipped
☐ Balls	☐ Lotto games
☐ Beads	☐ Musical instruments
☐ Blocks	☐ Paper
☐ Boats	☐ Pegboards
☐ Books	☐ Piano
☐ Cardboard Boxes	☐ Pounding boards
☐ Cars	☐ Puppets
☐ Clay	☐ Puzzles
☐ Climbing apparatus	☐ Records
☐ Cloth scraps	☐ Riding toys
☐ Clothes pins	☐ Slide
☐ Construction paper	☐ Spools
☐ Counting blocks	☐ Swings
☐ Crayons	☐ Telephones
☐ Dolls	☐ Tempera paints
☐ Doll beds and furniture	☐ Tools
☐ Doll carriage	☐ Tricycle
☐ Dramatic play props	☐ Trucks
☐ Dress-up clothing	☐ Water play

of behaviors on the checklist can be made in some logical order—perhaps the order in which the behaviors usually occur or in alphabetical order—to increase the efficiency of making the observations. (The Materials Available Checklist is one in which items are arranged alphabetically.)

Checklists are usually used when the teacher will have the opportunity to observe and prepare the checklist record for one pupil at a time. In this way the observer is able to mark the checklist immediately, as the behaviors occur. Another advantage to using a checklist for recording behavioral information is that, since the behaviors are written down in advance, the observer will probably not overlook some essential behavior. When you consider the extremely numerous and diverse behaviors likely to be exhibited by a group of learners during any single day, you can easily see that it would be quite possible to overlook many important behaviors if checklists were not used as record-keeping devices for observations.

Developing Checklists

The first step to follow in the development of a checklist is to consider the purposes involved in gathering the information. In most instances, this means that the starting point for the checklist will be the instructional or behavioral objectives set forth by the teacher or, in some cases, by the learners themselves. The objectives can be simply translated into the statements which will be included on the checklist. For example, if we have as an objective that a child will be able to choose independently and check out a library book, then the obvious statements to include on the checklist would be one statement about his selection of a book and another statement about his checking out the book: (1) chooses library book independently; and (2) follows correct procedure to check out library book.

It is important to describe clearly and concisely each of the specific actions expected to be observed in the learners. If care has been taken in formulating behavioral objectives, then it is quite likely that the translations of the objectives into statements for the checklist will result in clear statements. It is also possible to add statements to the checklists about variations or deviations which are likely to occur in whatever behaviors are to be observed (see Parts of Speech Usage Checklist, page 107). In this way, the efficiency of the observation is increased. Experience in working with children will indicate the areas in which difficulties or variations are likely to occur and the nature of the difficulties. These difficulties can then be translated into statements for the checklist so that variations or deviations from the anticipated behavior can be recorded, as well as instances of expected behavior. In this way, useful diagnostic information is likely to be recorded so that appropriate instructional decisions can be made.

Parts of Speech Usage Checklist

Date: _____

Name: _____

Observer: _____

Directions: There are pairs of items about each part of speech studied during the last unit in Language Arts class. Mark **one** in each pair of items to indicate whether the child uses the part of speech correctly **in casual conversation.**

The child uses:

1. Adjectives correctly _____

   Adjectives incorrectly _____

2. Adverbs correctly _____

   Adverbs incorrectly _____

3. Active verbs correctly _____

   Active verbs incorrectly _____

4. Passive verbs correctly _____

   Passive verbs incorrectly _____

5. Proper nouns correctly _____

   Proper nouns incorrectly _____

6. Common nouns correctly _____

   Common nouns incorrectly _____

7. Personal pronouns correctly _____

   Personal pronouns incorrectly _____

_____

Notice that this checklist was designed for use after a particular unit of instruction.

In many instances, information about the mere presence or absence of a behavior can be elaborated upon by indicating the sequence of occurrence of the behaviors or the dates of the exhibition of the behaviors. The listing of behaviors on the checklist should be in some logical order to increase the efficiency of the observation being made. The approximate order in which the behaviors are expected to occur is one appropriate method of determining how to list the behaviors. For those situations in which the learner's sequence of activities is important, the checklist can be set up so that *that* sequence of activities is clearly indicated, and numbers or letters placed next to each statement of the sequential activity expected. The Science Experiments Checklist on page 109 is an example of a useful means of noting sequential activities.

For some areas of the curriculum, growth toward specific learning outcomes may be somewhat slow and may occur over a fairly lengthy period of time. For these situations, the accounting can be made by inserting a date, instead of a check mark, next to the checklist's statement of the expected behavior (see the directions for completing the Primary Reading Checklist, page 110). In this way, the date goes beyond merely indicating the presence of that behavior. For these kinds of situations, the observer accomplishes more than merely jotting down a record of the behavior when it occurs—at some convenient time shortly thereafter, he will be able to reconstruct the sequence of the behaviors and, further, obtain an overview of the span of time consumed by the learners so observed. (Incidentally, cassette tape recorders are another means of reviewing and checklisting behaviors *after* their occurrence, at a convenient time.)

Another procedure, and one which we recommend, is to use the behavior tallying and charting procedures presented in Chapter Three to gather information which subsequently can be noted on a checklist. Frequency counts on behaviors could be taken until the criterion performance is reached and then the appropriate entry could be made on the checklist. For example, in order to exhibit the behavior defined by item 1 on the Primary Reading Checklist—"Listens to short stories (about five minutes duration) without interrupting"—a child may have to build up to this level of attending to stories. We, in turn, could record his day-to-day progress using behavior tallying procedures. Then, when he reaches the criterion defined by item 1, the date could be entered on the checklist.

PARTICIPATION CHARTS

Participation charts, although similar to checklists in that teachers usually use them to record the presence or absence of certain behaviors, are used when a number of

Science Experiments Checklist

Date: _____

Name: _____

Experiment: _____ *Measuring Volumes of Liquids* _____

Observer: _____

Directions: The items in the list are arranged in the order in which they are expected to be performed by students conducting the experiment. Indicate the order in which the student performed the behaviors by placing the numeral **one** next to the first behavior, **two** next to the second behavior, and so on. If a behavior was **not** performed, leave the space blank.

Sequence

_____ A. Reads statement of the problem to be studied.

_____ B. Assembles materials and equipment.

_____ C. Pours liquid into various graduated cylinders as per procedure outlined in lab manual.

_____ D. Notes the amount of liquid in 3 different graduate cylinders.

_____ E. Obtains feedback from peer checker regarding accuracy of measurement.

_____ F. Performs exercise of estimating volume in flask according to lab manual instructions.

_____ G. Checks estimates by measuring.

_____ H. Practices adding one drop of liquid at a time so that same number of drops are in each one.

_____ I. Prepares report of experiments and submits to instructor for feedback.

_____ J. Repeats any part of experiment if feedback indicates need for repetition to reach mastery.

Primary Reading Checklist

Name: _____

Observer: _____

Directions: Indicate when the behavior was observed to occur by placing the date in the blank next to the item. If the behavior is not observed, do not make any mark.

_____ 1. Listens to short stories (about five minutes duration) without interrupting

_____ 2. Uses simple sentences in his conversation

_____ 3. Tells about a sequence of three actions he has performed in correct order

_____ 4. Looks at picture books from front to back consistently

_____ 5. Looks at a row of written information from left to right

_____ 6. Follows a series of three directions given to him orally

_____ 7. Says letter names when shown cards with letters printed on them

_____ 8. Tells what will happen next in an unfinished story

_____ 9. Tells the main idea of a story after he has read it silently

_____ 10. Repeats short rhymes he has heard a number of times

_____ 11. Dictates his own three- or four-sentence story to the teacher

_____ 12. Illustrates his own stories appropriately

learners are being observed simultaneously and when their participation in some activity forms the purpose for making the observation. An obvious example of a situation in which it would be appropriate to use a participation chart is that of a group discussion. Other possible activities in which a participation chart is useful as a record-keeping device are included in the following discussion and samples of participation charts—again, used in the observation of a number of students at the same time.

Participation Chart A

Date: __5/18/73__

Activity: _____ _Science-Nature Hunt_ _____

Observer: _____ _V. Johnson_ _____

Name	Participates in Hunting	Contributes Specimens
Baker, S.	|||	|||
Ebbing, G.			
Grope, J.	ⅢⅡ	||
Hinkman, C.	||		
Kelly, B.	ⅢⅡ		||||
Nelson, F.		
Noone, C.			
Patras, P.	||		
Rich, C.	||||	|||
Roper, D.	ⅢⅡ |||	ⅢⅡ
Toth, T.		
Vincent, R.				

Developing Participation Charts

Participation charts are developed simply by listing the names of the learners and providing a space to tally *each* learner's participation (see Participation Chart A, above). One possible format would be to organize a chart into rows and columns. The names of the children could be entered in each row and the tally marks recorded in the columns as participation is exhibited by the individual child. There should be spaces on the record form to indicate the type of activity in which participation was desired, along with the time and the name of the observer, as shown in the sample participation charts which are given here.

For those activities in which children have a special seating arrangement, it is possible to design a map-like participation form along the lines of the seating chart. An example of this type of a form, Participation Chart B, is shown on page 112. In

Date: *12/7/73*

Activity: *Spelling Game*

Observer: *H. Wise*

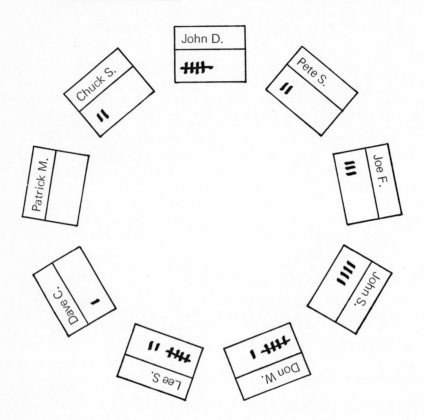

both participation charts, the observer simply tallies the number of times the child participates by making a single tally mark each time he observes a participation. The tally marks can later be added to determine the total number of participations during the activity.

If some indication of the *quality* of the participation is needed, a simple category or coding system can be developed so that, along with the number of participations, the quality of each participation can be recorded simultaneously. In these cases, it will not be possible to use a simple tally mark since different coding marks will be needed to indicate the various degrees of quality of the participation. This type of coding and recording on a participation chart will, of course, only be necessary in those instances when the quality as well as the participation itself are involved in the purpose for making the observation. In a group discussion situation, for example, three categories of contributions might be described: (1) a relevant contribution; (2) an irrelevant contribution; or (3) a neutral contribution. The symbol for *relevant contribution* might be a slash mark (/), for *irrelevant contribution* a small circle (o), and for *neutral contribution* a short horizontal line (-). The resulting participation chart might look like Participation Charts C and D, on pages 114 and 115.

In order to add efficiency to the observation process, it will be necessary to develop coding schemes which use symbols which can be written quickly. A code which had to be recorded by using a dot inside a triangle (△) would be somewhat inefficient since it would take the observer a lot of time, compared to the time it takes to make a tally mark, to make the recording. Of course, in those instances where simple coding schemes are developed to indicate the quality of the participation, participation charts become a slight variation of rating scales.

RATING SCALES

Rating scales are similar to checklists in that they are used when the behaviors to be exhibited are known in advance, but they exceed the limits of the checklist when there is the added need to record frequency and/or quality characteristics of behaviors. As is the case with checklists, rating scales help focus the observer's attention on specific behaviors, and they tend to encourage precision in the observation process.

Uses of Rating Scales

Whenever it is appropriate to the purpose for which the observation is being made and where it is possible to determine the *extent* to which a particular quality is present, rating scales can be used. Usually, rating scales are used in situations where the performance to be observed has several different aspects or components and where each component will be rated on a separate scale or dimension. A rating scale is, in a way, an extension of a checklist in that the behaviors to be observed are listed and an opportunity is provided to indicate the *degree* to which a behavior occurs—the frequency of the behavior—and, also, there is opportunity to indicate the quality characteristics of the performance.

Date: 4/23/73

Activity: *Social Studies Group Discussion*

Observer: *C. Becker*

Name													Total Contributions	Total Relevant Contributions
Abel, Sam	/	/	/	–									4	3
Corning, Ellen													0	0
Cotl, Charles	–	–	/	–									4	1
Davidson, Mary	/	/	/	/	/	0	/	–					8	6
Feathers, Mary	0	/											2	1
Horn, Peter	/	/	/	/									4	4
Jacob, Jane	–	/	/	–									4	2
Moore, Susan	/	/	/	/	/	/							6	6
Motter, James	0	0	0										3	0
Smith, John	–	–	/	–									4	1
Tate, Deborah													0	0
Walker, James	/												1	1

Code: / = relevant contribution   – = neutral contribution

O = irrelevant contribution   No mark indicates no contribution

The typical rating scale record form consists of a listing of behaviors, and components or aspects of these behaviors which are to be rated by the observer, and some type of scale for indicating the degree to which the behavior is present. In other words, the rating scale is simply a device for systematically recording observers' judgments about a performance. Because judgments must be made, there are many possibilities for error. The major difference between a checklist and a rating scale is that the observer is merely indicating presence or absence of a

Participation Chart D

Date: 11/5/73

Activity: Group Project

Observer: D. Bloom

Name

Name														
Carroll, J.	1	1	1	1										
Davids, O.	1													
Greer, J.	0	0	0											
Lewis, K.	1	1	1	0	1									
Masters, D.	1	1	1	1	1									
Sedman, D.	0	1	1											
Sobel, D.	0	0	0											
Walker, G.	1	1	1	1	1	1								
Young, M.	1	1												

Code: 1 = facilitating contribution 0 = interfering contribution

behavior with a checklist, and he is indicating his judgment about the frequency and/or quality characteristics of the performance when he uses a rating scale.

The aspects or dimensions of the performance used on the rating scale should be derived from the purpose for the observation and should be such that they are directly observable. Since there seems to be a tendency to develop rating scales for areas in which there isn't ample opportunity to make necessary observations, use of rating scales should be confined to situations in which the observer is detached enough from the activity in which the subject of the observation is engaged so that the observer can concentrate and control his judgment.

When properly developed, rating scales have several important advantages. They can direct observation toward specific, and clearly stated, dimensions of a behavior. They can provide a common ground for comparing children on similar behaviors if comparison is a part of the teacher's purpose for decision making. Rating scales also provide a convenient way of recording judgments of observers. Since it is possible for several observers to use the same form and make records for a given child simultaneously, there is the possibility of pooling the ratings and obtaining an average rating on the pupil's performance. This tends to decrease the biases of individual observers and increase objectivity. In the final analysis, however, it must be remembered that the nature of a rating scale is such that observers must make judgments.

Developing Rating Scales

The two major components of any rating scale are the list of dimensions of the behavior(s) which will be rated and the scale(s) which will be used to rate each of the behaviors. We will see that in some types of rating scales it will be necessary to use the same scale over and over again to judge all of the dimensions of all the behaviors. In other types of rating scales, the scale used to make a judgment of the dimension of the behavior will change for each new dimension of the behavior. The first step then in constructing any kind of rating scale is to prepare a list of the important features of the behavior which are to be judged. We have already referred to these as components or dimensions of the behavior. For teachers, the obvious starting point is to consider the statement of behavioral objectives as a means of generating a listing of behaviors and behavior dimensions. For some behavioral objectives, it may be necessary to list several dimensions of the behavior and for other objectives, the statement of the behavior as it exists in the objective may be unidimensional and adequate.

The type of scale to use in rating the behaviors should be determined on the basis of the purpose for the observation. The scale will need to be translated into a continuum on which are represented various degrees of quality and/or frequency for the performance. The continuum may be divided into a number of different parts, in which case the rater is forced to choose a specific point along the continuum; or the continuum may be constructed in such a way that the rater is allowed to indicate his rating at any point along the continuum. In any case, each category along the continuum should be defined as specifically as possible according to the purpose of the observation.

As has been our concern with other types of recording devices, the dimensions of the behavior which are to be rated should be stated such that they are directly observable. We will see that some types of rating scales provide better opportunities to meet this criterion than others. Another general consideration in constructing rating scales is to be sure that the listing of behavior dimensions represents items which are *unidimensional*—that is, only one component of a behavior is involved for any given rating. If a rater has to consider two components of a behavior simultaneously, he is never quite sure how much weight to give the various components and, as a result, his rating loses objectivity.

Several other general considerations, which are likely to improve the objectivity and the reliability of rating scales as recording devices for observation, are as follows: (1) It is often a good idea to provide a space for comments after each behavior dimension; in this way, the rater is able to note reasons for making certain ratings. This is somewhat similar to an anecdotal record. (2) A space or entry should be provided which enables a rater to indicate that he hasn't had adequate opportunities to observe a given behavior dimension. These additions to the rating scale, which add clarity to the record, are worth consideration as the various types of rating scales are developed and field tested. The space for extra comments of an anecdotal nature may be particularly useful later on when evaluating the scales.

Constant Alternatives Scales

As stated earlier, there are several types of scales which are available and the type to be used in any given situation should be chosen on the basis of the purpose for the observation. Several different types of scales, relevant to the situations described in the examples, will be included in this chapter. Scales in which the same set of alternatives are used to rate every dimension of the behavior are termed *constant alternatives scales.* These constant alternatives may take different forms of descriptors, such as *always, sometimes, never,* or *good, fair, poor*; or they may take the form of numerical ratings, numbers ranging from 1 to 5 with 1 being coded as *seldom* and 5 being coded as *almost always*, or 1 being coded as *poor* and 5 being coded as *excellent.* The Project Activities Rating Scale, on page 118, is an example of a constant alternatives scale, using as it does the same set of descriptors for each behavior dimension. The type of descriptors or the number scale used is not as important as the fact that the constant alternatives scale is not expected to yield results which are as objective as those scales which include more specific descriptors of the behavior dimensions to be rated.

Changing Alternatives Scales

Rating scales in which different sets of alternatives are used to rate the different behavior dimensions are termed *changing alternatives rating scales.* In this case, of course, we have the opposite of a constant alternatives scale. For certain of the behavior dimensions listed on the rating scale, one kind of alternative might be used, and for other behavior dimensions, another alternative. A simple illustration of this might be a situation in which some of the behavior dimensions involve a quality rating. For the frequency dimensions, we might want to use alternatives such as *always, sometimes,* and *never,* and for the quality dimensions, we might use a set of alternatives such as *poor, fair,* and *good.* Whenever we mix up the alternatives used to describe the rating continuum within the same rating scale, we have developed the type of rating scale called a changing alternatives scale. The

Project Activities Rating Scale

Date: _____

Name: _____

Observer: _____

Description of Project Activity: _____

_____

Directions: For each item, circle the word which best describes the child's performance on that item. **N/O** = no opportunity to observe.

1. Is the child prepared for the meetings of the group?   Never   Usually   Always   N/O

2. Does the child show an interest in the project?   Never   Usually   Always   N/O

3. Does the child participate in making plans for the next steps?   Never   Usually   Always   N/O

4. Does the child cause other children to become interested in the project?   Never   Usually   Always   N/O

5. Does the child engage in behaviors which disrupt the group activities?   Never   Usually   Always   N/O

6. Does the child contribute ideas during group meetings?   Never   Usually   Always   N/O

7. Does the child contribute materials during group meetings?   Never   Usually   Always   N/O

8. Does the child exhibit any commitment to the project above and beyond the scheduled group activities?   Never   Usually   Always   N/O

Use the space below to make any other comments you feel are important considerations when interpreting this rating scale.

Language Performance Rating Scale, below, developed for use at the intermediate grade level, is an example of a changing alternatives type of rating scale; only a sampling of the items needed for a complete assessment are shown in the example.

Numerical Rating Scales

Some rating scales are called *numerical rating scales.* Usually numerical rating scales are also constant alternatives type; however, it is possible to change the alternatives

Language Performance

Intermediate Level

Date: _____

Name: _____

Observer: _____

Directions: Circle the word which best describes your judgment about the learner's performance on that item.

1. When speaking before the class, does the child hold the interest of the group?

Always Boring	Usually Interesting	Always Interesting	N/O

2. Does the child use language appropriate for his age level?

Hardly Ever	Usually	Almost Always	N/O

3. Is the child's speech clear and distinct?

Unintelligible	Usually Clear	Very Clear	N/O

4. When speaking before the group, is the child relaxed?

Very Nervous	Little Nervous	Very Relaxed	N/O

5. Does the child choose vocabulary to best express his thoughts?

Inappropriate	Usually Well Chosen	Very Appropriate	N/O

6. What is the overall impression made by the child when speaking before the group?

Very Poor	Fair	Excellent	N/O

Comments:

Role-Playing by Young Children

Date:_____

Name:_____

Observer:_____

Directions: Indicate your rating of the child's role-playing behaviors
by circling the number of your rating.

Key: 5 = excellent
1 = very poor
N/O = no opportunity to observe

1. How does the child perform a role
   when he has had an opportunity to
   plan for it ahead of time?   1   2   3   4   5   N/O

2. How does the child perform a role
   when he has had no opportunity to
   plan ahead (the situation occurs
   spontaneously)?   1   2   3   4   5   N/O

3. How well does the child use
   appropriate vocabulary for his role? 1   2   3   4   5   N/O

4. How well does the child use
   appropriate actions for his role?   1   2   3   4   5   N/O

5. How well does the child use
   appropriate props for his role?   1   2   3   4   5   N/O

6. How well does the child respond to
   the words and actions of the others
   involved in the role playing?   1   2   3   4   5   N/O

Comments:

and produce a numerical rating scale which is of the changing alternatives type. In
using a numerical rating scale, the rater or observer simply checks or circles a
number to indicate the degree to which a behavior is present or to indicate the
degree of quality present in the behavior performance. Usually each of the numbers
in the series is given a verbal description so that the rater is sure of the meanings of
the number codes. Sometimes, however, the observer is merely informed that the
largest number refers to a high rating, the lowest number refers to a low rating, and

the other numbers represent intermediate values. In the example on page 120, Role-Playing by Young Children, only the end points of the scale have been described and the rater would have to use his own judgment about what constitutes the intermediate points. We will see that, often, describing only the end points of the scale is possible when developing a numerical scale or when developing some other types of descriptive rating scales—especially graphic rating scales.

Simple Graphic Rating Scales

A *simple graphic sacle* is one in which a line is drawn and points along the line are identified. The rater is allowed to mark anywhere along the line, even between the points which have been identified. It is possible that only the end points of the graph or line will be described. In this case, the observer is given only a minimum amount of guidance in making his ratings. The end-point descriptors on the graph indicate to the observer what he *ought* to consider, but leaves the decision regarding what constitutes intermediate degrees of the performance to the observer. The "graphic" part of the simple graphic rating scale consists of a simple horizontal line.

Whenever the *categories* marked along the continuum or graph are the *same* for each behavior dimension, the rating scale—even though it is a graphic rating scale—would be called a constant alternatives type of rating scale. It is fairly easy to change a simple descriptive or a numerical scale into a simple graphic scale by adding a horizontal line, or graph, to the existing scale. The example of a simple graphic scale shown on page 122 is really a modification (insertion of the horizontal line) of the Project Activities Rating Scale used earlier (see page 118).

Descriptive Graphic Rating Scales

A type of rating scale in which each of the degrees of quality or frequency are specifically described in extensive behavioral terms is called a *specific descriptive rating scale.* These types of rating scales are almost always of the changing alternatives type of rating scale. One of the problems involved in using a specific descriptive rating scale is that there is no way to indicate a rating which might lie somewhere between two adjacent descriptions of a behavior. It is possible to combine the specific descriptive rating scale with the graphic rating scale to produce a type of rating scale which is called a descriptive graphic rating scale, since the descriptive graphic rating scale handles the problem of not being able to mark between two adjacent behavior descriptions. In general, the descriptive graphic scale is the most desirable type of scale to use because the specific descriptions needed to develop it generally lead to clearer and more unidimensional behavior statements. (Examples of descriptive graphic rating scale items are included on page 124.) The results yielded through the use of the descriptive graphic rating scale are generally the most objective information available through the use of rating scales to record observations.

Project Activities Rating Scale

Date: _____

Name: _____

Observer: _____

Description of Project Activity: _____

_____

Directions: Place a check mark at any point along the line to indicate your judgment of the child's performance on that item. If you have had insufficient opportunities to observe the child, circle **N/O.**

1. Is the child prepared for the meetings of the group?

   N/O

   Never   Usually   Always

2. Does the child show an interest in the project?

   N/O

   Never   Usually   Always

3. Does the child participate in making plans for the next steps?

   N/O

   Never   Usually   Always

4. Does the child cause other children to become interested in the project?

   N/O

   Never   Usually   Always

5. Does the child engage in behaviors which disrupt the group activities?

   N/O

   Never   Usually   Always

6. Does the child contribute ideas during group meetings?

N/O

Never   Usually   Always

7. Does the child contribute materials during group meetings?

N/O

Never   Usually   Always

8. Does the child exhibit any commitment to the project above and beyond the scheduled group activities?

N/O

Never   Usually   Always

Comments:

SUMMARY

Three types of record forms used in observation were presented in detail in this chapter, along with suggestions for developing and using them—checklists, participation charts, and rating scales.

The checklist consists of a list of statements about behaviors which are expected to be displayed. For each statement, there is a way to indicate whether or not the behavior was present during the observation. Checklists should be used when the behaviors to be exhibited are known in advance and when there is no need to provide information about the frequency and/or quality characteristics of the behaviors.

Participation charts are similar to checklists in that the presence or absence of behavior is indicated, but they differ from checklists in that they are used to record the behaviors of many learners simultaneously and used when participation in some activity is the purpose for the observation. Most participation charts consist of a listing of the names of the people involved in the activity and a place to make tally marks every time a participation is made.

Rating scales are similar to checklists in that they are used when the behaviors to be exhibited are known in advance, but they are better utilized when there is the added need to have a record of frequency and/or quality characteristics of the behaviors. Usually, rating scales are used in situations where the performance to be observed has several different dimensions and where each dimension will be rated on a separate scale. Rating scales can take many forms; there are constant alterna-

Sample Items for Descriptive Graphic Rating Scales

Note: Raters may mark anywhere along the line.

To what extent is the child interested in books?

|—————————————————————————————————|

| Handles books carelessly; never chooses books during free activity time; does not join group for stories | Handles books carefully; is curious about contents of books; sometimes chooses activities involving books | Handles books very carefully; knows books by their titles; engages in some free choice activity with books almost every day |

To what extent does the child listen attentively?

|—————————————————————————————————|

| Never listens; looks around, gets up and walks away when someone talks to him | Sits fairly still and listens for at least five minutes; looks at speaker during this time | Is very attentive in listening situations; facial expressions indicate careful listening; no obvious fidgeting while listening |

To what extent does the child participate in art activities?

|—————————————————————————————————|

| Never chooses art activities during free activity periods; makes verbal statements about lack of interest in art | Participates in most available art activities; usually avoids activities he considers messy; is occasionally reluctant to display his work | Enthusiastically participates in all available art activities; shows his products with pride |

tives, changing alternatives, numerical, simple descriptive, simple graphic, or descriptive graphic types of rating scales.

ACTIVITY 1

1. Choose an area of teaching which you wish to learn more about. Some suggestions are: methods of presenting lessons, ways of helping learners operate independently, types of materials and their arrangement, techniques of questioning, or types of reinforcement.

2. Develop a checklist to gather information about the area you've chosen.

3. Try out your checklist through observation in a classroom. As you try the checklist, keep notes about any problems you experience and use this information to revise your checklist.

4. Share your revised checklist with a colleague, whose reaction may lead you to make further revisions.

ACTIVITY 2

Use the participation chart on page 127 to test your skill in observing several learners simultaneously.

ACTIVITY 3

Here's an experience which will allow you to use a rating scale that has already been developed and to revise an existing rating scale. Here's how to proceed:

1. Use the Teacher Behavior Rating Scale shown on page 129 as you observe a teacher in a classroom situation.

2. On the basis of your experiences with this rating scale, revise the rating scale so that it is a descriptive graphic scale. Add or delete items as you deem necessary.

3. Field test *your* descriptive graphic version of the Teacher Behavior Rating Scale.

Participation Chart

Date:_____

*Activity:*_____

*Observer:*_____

Name

_____

_____

_____

_____

_____

_____

_____

_____

_____

_____

_____

_____

_____

Codes:

Teacher Behavior Rating Scale

Date:_____

*Name of Teacher:*_____

*Observer:*_____

Directions: Circle the word which best describes your judgment of performance on the behavior in question. Circle **N/O** if you had no opportunity to observe the behavior.

1. How often does the teacher talk about behavioral evidence of children's characteristics?   Hardly Ever   Sometimes   Frequently   N/O

2. To what extent does the teacher change grouping for different activities?   Hardly Ever   Sometimes   Frequently   N/O

3. To what extent does the teacher engage in assessment procedures which are beyond those routinely required?   Hardly Ever   Sometimes   Frequently   N/O

4. How well does the teacher relate methods of teaching to characteristics of the learners?   Poor   Fair   Very Good   N/O

5. How well does the teacher relate educational materials to the characteristics of the learners?   Poor   Fair   Very Good   N/O

6. To what extent does the teacher exhibit a positive approach to managing children's behavior?   Hardly Ever   Sometimes   Frequently   N/O

7. To what extent does the teacher use the services of available resource people?   Hardly Ever   Sometimes   Frequently   N/O

8. How well does the teacher communicate with the learners?   Poor   Fair   Very Good   N/O

9. How well does the teacher assess learners' achievements of objectives?   Poor   Fair   Very Good   N/O

10. How well has the teacher organized the environment so that learners have easy access to materials?   Poor   Fair   Very Good   N/O

11. How well does the teacher communicate
with other professionals with whom he
comes in contact?   Poor   Fair   Very Good   N/O

Comments:

FIVE

Anecdotal records

This chapter is about another type of record form for observations—the anecdotal record. When you complete this chapter and the recommended activities, you should be able to:

1. Differentiate between appropriate and inappropriate uses of anecdotal records
2. Prepare anecdotal records which are factual accounts of incidents
3. Summarize and draw conclusions based on a series of anecdotal records
4. Devise a systematic procedure so that anecdotal records will be prepared periodically for all children in a group and for a representative sample of their behavior

Anecdotal records are exactly as the name suggests—they are records of anecdotes, brief accounts of some event that happened. An anecdotal record might be thought of as a "word picture" of an incident, behavior, or event that occurred. It is important to emphasize that anecdotal records should be *factual* descriptions of the incidents that have been observed. Of the anecdotal records on the following page, Anecdotal Record Form A is a factual description, while Anecdotal Record

Anecdotal Record Form A

Learner: _____ Jay Samuels _____ Date: _May 24, 1973_

Observer: _____ L. Martin _____ Time: _9:15 a.m._

Incident: *Jay was playing with blocks. Hank came over and picked up a*
truck which was near Jay's block construction. Jay hit Hank
and said, "No, no, no!" Hank put down the truck and walked
away.

Anecdotal Record Form B

Learner: _____ Jay Samuels _____ Date: _May 24, 1973_

Observer: _____ L. Martin _____ Time: _9:15 a.m._

Incident: *Jay was (happily) playing with blocks. Hank came skipping*
(merrily) over and picked up a truck which was near Jay's
block construction. Jay (clobbered) Hank and (screamed)
"No, no, no!" Hank (reluctantly) put down the truck and
walked away.

Form B is not. The words which should *not* have been used in form B are circled. You will find us emphasizing the factual nature of anecdotal records continually in this chapter.

Use for Unanticipated Behaviors

It has already been indicated that some types of record forms are more appropriate to some observation purposes than others. In the case of anecdotal records, they are best used to record observations of unanticipated behaviors, incidents, or events. Children behave spontaneously in many ways which are not anticipated or expected by the teacher, and the anecdotal record provides a method of recording the observations of these spontaneous behaviors.

Since the observer is dealing with spontaneous, unexpected behaviors, the type of record used for observations of this nature is not highly structured—nor can it be. For the anecdotal record, the only preplanning possible is the preparation of a general format with labels for items such as the date, time, name of learner, and so on. Other than general format decisions, little preplanning is possible for anecdotal records.

In instances where behavior can be anticipated in advance, generally it would be inappropriate to attempt to record behaviors using anecdotal records—for example, consider the anecdotal record below. It includes some information which

Learner:	*Ann Martin*	Date:	*5/7/73*
Observer:	*P. Orr*	Time:	*10:15 a.m.*
Setting:	*Reading*		

Incident: During reading class, Ann pronounced the word fieldhouse *correctly.*

Is this report cross-filed?   **Yes**____ **No**____

could have been anticipated in advance. This teacher should have reasoned that this behavior is one likely to occur in reading class; and, if it is considered important to record it, the teacher should also include it on a checklist.

Just because we have said that anecdotal records are to be used for reporting unanticipated behaviors, the reader should not conclude that anecdotal records are unimportant. Neither the anecdotal records nor the behaviors and incidents included in them are insignificant. One important point to remember is that these unanticipated behaviors are not likely to be included on any other kinds of records (because of the preplanning involved in designing other types of records) and, if it were not for the anecdotal record, this information would probably be lost, or at least recalled inaccurately. On the other hand, there is no advantage in using anecdotal records to obtain information for those purposes where other record forms are required.

PREPARING ANECDOTAL RECORDS—
AN INTRODUCTION

The most important statement which can be given about the preparation of anecdotal records is that the individual preparing the record, the observer, should state exactly what happened in clear, concise language and should make the statement or the report at the time the observation is occurring, if at all possible. Each anecdotal record should be limited to a description of one specific incident.

If more than one child is involved in the incident, then separate records should be written for each of the children involved. Consider the sample anecdotal record on page 135. Both Pete and Larry were involved in a single incident. Having filled in the format data and described the incident concisely, it is possible for the observer to duplicate the single record, change the duplicate's *Name* entry (from *Pete Brock* to *Larry Watkins*), and file it with each child's set of records so that the incident is included with each child's other behaviors and can be interpreted in light of his overall pattern of behavior. In using carbon paper or a copying machine, then "whiting out" or otherwise changing the name, the teacher would *not* need to rewrite completely a duplicate record for Larry.

In cases of duplicated anecdotal records, there should be a record made of the fact that the report is cross-filed. One way to handle this is to add the line "Is this report cross-filed?   Yes_____ No_____" to the anecdotal record format. Usually, one child will stand out or play a major role in the incident, and, in these cases, the observer should concentrate on the activities of this one child and, of course, prepare one anecdotal record for that child.

```
Name:              Pete Brock              Date:      3/18/73

Observer:          C. Jones               Time:      12:50 p.m.

Setting:           Playground
```

Incident: *Pete and Larry were swinging. Pete was pushing Larry. Larry said, "You're pushing too high." Pete said, "No, you're just a scaredy-cat." Larry started crying and said, "Stop pushing me." Pete said, "Scaredy-cat, scaredy-cat." Then some other children came and asked Pete to play ball. He went away with them. Larry continued crying for several minutes.*

Is this report cross-filed?   Yes ✓ No_____

While it may not always be possible to prepare the anecdotal record as the behavior occurs, the record should be written out as soon as possible after the behavior is observed. In general, the less the delay, the more accurate the record is likely to be. Teachers might consider the use of simple audio recording devices such as cassette tape recorders, which could be used to keep a verbatim account of the incident as it is occurring, or very soon after it occurs they could recite the incident. In this way, the audio tapes could be transcribed later to anecdotal record forms, which could be filed with the other forms for that learner. The use of an audio recording device, if close at hand, would be somewhat more efficient than having the teacher take the time to write out the anecdote as it occurs.

Be Factual

We discussed observer's biases in Chapter Two. Since anecdotal records are open-ended, there are numerous opportunities for the observer's biases to be reflected in the anecdotal record. Biases can creep in when selecting behaviors to record. We must monitor our feelings so that we do not needlessly focus on behaviors which are especially noxious to us. These behaviors may represent a "hang-up" for us, but constitute no problem for the child. We must also exercise caution not to choose to record behaviors which are atypical for the child. In fact, it may be a good practice *not* to record an unusual behavior the *first* time it is seen. If it is seen again there is some indication that it wasn't a once-in-a-lifetime occurrence and it could be recorded at that time.

Only those statements which are a specific description of what actually occurred should be used in the anecdotal record. (Even if the child says, "He's a stinky old teacher," we should record the child's subjective comment.) Of course, we can never make an anecdotal record completely free of the biases of the observer who is preparing it. This is so partly because of the richness of the English language. Each observer is likely to choose slightly different terms to describe what is going on and these terms, when read by others, may be interpreted in ways slightly different from the way in which the original observer intended. Consider, for example, the possible ways of reporting that a child talked. We could write simply, "He said," or we might write any of a score of other words: *screamed, shouted, yelled, whispered, commented, chattered, uttered, remarked, intoned,* and so on—each has connotations that can be interpreted in various ways by those who read the anecdotal record.

So, even when we try to make our report factual, the choice of words may call for an interpretation—or create a misinterpretation. One way of avoiding this problem is to choose one word or phrase and use it all the time. For example, every time you need to report that someone talked, use the word *said.* This practice will serve to eliminate some of the subjectivity involved in preparing anecdotal records.

Another way to partially circumvent the possible bias that may creep in, even when the observer tries very hard to prepare a bias-free record, is to provide supporting information in the way of samples of work, tape recordings, snapshots, and so forth. These kinds of supporting evidence are, when taken together with the anecdotal record, less subject to varying interpretations than an anecdotal record standing alone.

INTERPRETING ANECDOTAL RECORDS

The act of interpreting anecdotal records should be kept clearly separate from the actual recording of the incident, and the interpretation should not be made until several anecdotes are available for perusal. Other authors suggest that an "interpretation" portion of the anecdotal record be included on the same form, but that it be clearly marked as an interpretation and somehow separated from the rest of the form. Such an anecdotal record might look like the one for Judy Smith on page 137.

```
┌─────────────────────────────────────────────────────────────┐
│                                                             │
│   Name: _____ Judy Smith _____   Date: __ 3/5/73 __ │
│   Observer: _____ G. Stephens _____  Time: _ 2:00 p.m. _│
│                                                             │
│   Incident: Judy arrived late for school this morning. She  │
│             said nothing when she did arrive. During recess │
│             I heard her say to Mamie, "I try so hard to     │
│             walk fast but I'm just slower than the other    │
│             kids on my block."                              │
│                                                             │
│   Interpretation: Judy has been late several times in the   │
│                   past month. She seems mad at herself for  │
│                   being late.                               │
│                                                             │
└─────────────────────────────────────────────────────────────┘
```

Reviewing *several* anecdotal records which have been *prepared over a period of time* for the same pupil, the teacher is better able to determine if the behaviors recorded represent typical or atypical behaviors for that child. It is difficult to make specific interpretations for each and every separate anecdote, and it is our position that better interpretations can be made when several anecdotes are considered together. For purposes of clarity, then, it makes good sense to summarize anecdotes and make interpretations and recommendations on forms which are completely separate from the anecdotal record forms themselves.

A Pause for an Example

Here and on the following pages (138-140), we have provided a series of five sample anecdotal records for one learner, leading to an example Anecdotal Record Summary (page 141), a useful interpretation and recommendation form. After reviewing the child's anecdotal records, the teacher concluded that Mike was avoiding situations requiring reading. The teacher's recommendations are really a brief listing of some instructional decisions which were then made. Apparently, the teacher will conduct some further observations, and make a referral if necessary, to determine if Mike has a vision problem. The teacher also plans to design some instructional procedures so Mike will gain rewards in reading situations.

Anecdotal Record 1

Name: _____ *Mike Solt* _____ Date: _____ *2/6/73* _____

Observer: _____ *C. Seaver* _____ Time: _____ *10:15 a.m.* _____

Setting: _____ *Reading* _____

Incident: *When asked to find a book to read independently, Mike went to his seat and put his head down on his desk.*

Anecdotal Record 2

Name: _____ *Mike Solt* _____ Date: _____ *2/10/73* _____

Observer: _____ *C. Seaver* _____ Time: _____ *1:45 p.m.* _____

Setting: _____ *Social Studies Project* _____

Incident: *Sam asked Mike to go look up the spelling of the word thruway for their map project. Mike said, "I'm too busy with this bridge. Get Carol to do it."*

Anecdotal Record 3

Name: _____Mike Solt_____ Date: _2/16/73_

Observer: _____C. Seaver_____ Time: _1:00 p.m._

Setting: _____Library_____

Incident: Mike remained in the classroom when all the other children
went for a library period.

Anecdotal Record 4

Name: _____Mike Solt_____ Date: _2/20/73_

Observer: _____C. Seaver_____ Time: _11:10 a.m._

Setting: _____Reading_____

Incident: When asked to read a paragraph orally, Mike said, "I don't
feel good. Can I go lay down?"

Name: _____ *Mike Solt* _____ Date: _ *2/25/73* _

Observer: _____ *C. Seaver* _____ Time: _ *2:20 p.m.* _

Setting: _____ *Free Activity* _____

Incident: *Mike asked Joe for some information on locomotives. Joe said, "There's a good book on that over on my desk." Mike said, "Hey, why don't you just tell me what it says?"*

Be Purposeful

Even though anecdotal records provide a way of keeping track of unanticipated behaviors, the observer should record incidents with a purpose. It is impossible to record all unanticipated behaviors, and since some selection of behavior to record will be necessary, the selection should be done in terms of some instructional decisions that need to be made about the pupil, some goal or other purpose for the observation needing to be fulfilled.

Be Systematic

The task of keeping anecdotal records for all of the children for whom a teacher is responsible may seem to be insurmountable. The trick in handling the volume of anecdotal records which will be needed is to work out some kind of a pattern for collecting records about children. This kind of pattern also has the advantage of insuring that no children will be overlooked. For example, a teacher may decide that he will always prepare at least one anecdotal record for some child during a free play period, an oral reading period, or during a recess period—or whatever the period in which he finds himself with free time to record incidents while children are engaged in independent activities.

Anecdotal Record Summary

Name: _Mike Solt_____

Observer(s): _C. Seaver_____

_____

_____

This summary is based on _____5_____ records taken from
                (no. of records)

           _2/6/73_____ to ____2/25/73____
             (date)   (date)

Is there supporting information on file?   Yes_____ No _✓_

If yes, where is the information located? _____

_____

What supporting information is available? _____

_____

Summary Statements: Mike avoids situations involving reading. His past
        reading achievement scores are okay. We have some
        evidence that he can read.

Recommendations:
    1. Try to make reading a rewarding experience.
    2. Do some checking to see if he might be having trouble
       with his vision.

Of course, the choice of period may be dictated by the knowledge that some behaviors are much more likely to occur at given times during the day than at others. If the teacher is interested in children's social-emotional behaviors, then he might be especially prepared to keep anecdotal records during an independent study or recess period when children are likely to make spontaneous contacts with other children.

Another way to set up a pattern for keeping anecdotal records is to decide to observe a certain number of children each day and simply rotate through the class roster so that each child is being observed every fifth or every eighth day, or whatever the pattern worked out. This method of using a system to continually keep anecdotal records does not preclude the teacher from keeping an extra record now and then for a child who exhibits some unusually interesting unexpected behavior. For example, the teacher may not intend to keep an anecdotal record on Charles until next Thursday; but if, on Monday, Charles makes an unusual social contact with a child with whom he has never before interacted, the teacher may decide that that is significant enough for an anecdotal record to be made for Charles on Monday, even though another pupil may have been designated for that day.

ANECDOTAL RECORD FORMATS

It was mentioned earlier that anecdotal records are used to record unanticipated behaviors and that the only type of preplanning possible is the preparation of a general format for the record keeping. One advantage of having a general format prepared ahead of time is that important information is not likely to be forgotten. If a teacher is using blank sheets of paper or blank index cards on which to record anecdotes, he is much more likely to behave unsystematically in his recording of his observations than if he uses some kind of preplanned anecdotal record form. When the anecdotal record format is being designed, the need to file the records should be kept in mind. For this reason, it may be desirable to prepare the form and mimeograph it on 4×6 or 5×8 index cards which can be easily filed alphabetically for children and then chronologically for each child. If index cards are used, the summary and recommendations component form could be mimeographed on a different color index card for easy accessibility.

Another type of anecdotal record form might be designed to be mimeographed on standard 8½ × 11 paper. These records could then be filed in manila filing folders, with each pupil having his own folder. The folders would probably be arranged in alphabetical order and the anecdotal records in each folder could be arranged in chronological order. The use of manila folders does provide more space for storing supplementary information such as samples of work, drawings, snapshots, tapes, and so on.

What to Include

There is not much room for variation in the format for anecdotal records since there are certain items that must be included. However, the specific arrangement of the information is a matter of personal preference. Having the child's name and the date at the top of the form seems to make filing easier.

Whatever type of form is developed, several items are important for inclusion: the *name of the child* and the *name of the observer*; the *date* and the *time* at which the incident occurred; a space for a *description of the incident* itself; and space to indicate the *setting* in which the event occurred. Notice that in the sample anecdotal record forms we have provided near the end of the chapter (pages 145-153), a means of indicating whether or not supporting information is available has also been planned for. Also, at the end of the chapter (page 155), a sample form for summarizing a number of anecdotal records about the same child and for making interpretations and recommendations, has been included. Our suggested anecdotal record forms do not include spaces on the form itself for interpretation of the behavior since it is our contention that teachers are seldom in a position to make an interpretation on the basis of a single anecdote. If a teacher decides to develop his own form, or to adapt one of those presented here, it is important to try out the form in a field test and make necessary revisions before multiple copies are produced and made available. (Some observers may find the placement of certain kinds of information easier to record if they are on one part of the form than on another.) This is probably a matter of individual style and preference.

SUMMARY

Anecdotal records are brief accounts of incidents and behaviors. They should be factual descriptions and should be used for recording information about unanticipated behaviors.

The exact format of the record form may vary, but certain items should be included: name of the child, name of the observer, date, time, setting, and a description of the incident. It was recommended that single incidents *not* be interpreted. A summary form for use in summarizing and interpreting a series of anecdotal records was presented.

ACTIVITY 1

We've talked about using observation methods to gather the information needed to make instructional decisions, and in Chapter One we listed ten classes of instructional decisions with which teachers have to deal. In this chapter, we indicated anecdotal records should be used for recording unanticipated behaviors. Observe some unanticipated instructional decision-making behaviors *exhibited by teachers.* Record your observations on the forms provided (pages 145-153).

ACTIVITY 2

1. Develop an anecdotal record-keeping form, or use the format provided on the following pages.
2. Collect a series of anecdotes for the same child over a period of about two weeks (or collect your anecdotes about a teacher).
3. Gather any supporting information if it is available.
4. Complete the Anecdotal Record Summary (page 155) based on the set of anecdotal records you gathered. If colleagues have anecdotes on the same child (or teacher), share them with each other and then check later to see if you essentially agree on the summary statement and recommendations.

Name: _____ *Date:* _____

Observer: _____ *Time:* _____

Setting: _____

Incident:

Is this report cross-filed?   Yes _____ No _____

Is supporting information available?   Yes _____ No _____

What is it? _____ Where is it? _____

Name:_____   Date:_____

Observer:_____   Time:_____

Setting: _____

Incident:

Is this report cross-filed?   Yes_____No_____

Is supporting information available?   Yes_____No_____

What is it?_____Where is it?_____

Name: _____   *Date:* _____

Observer: _____   *Time:* _____

Setting: _____

Incident:

Is this report cross-filed?   **Yes** _____ **No** _____

Is supporting information available?   **Yes** _____ **No** _____

What is it?_____Where is it?_____

Name: _____   *Date:* _____

Observer: _____   *Time:* _____

Setting: _____

Incident:

Is this report cross-filed?   Yes_____ No_____

Is supporting information available?   Yes_____ No_____

What is it?_____Where is it?_____

Name: _____   *Date:* _____

Observer: _____   *Time:* _____

Setting: _____

Incident:

Is this report cross-filed?   **Yes**_____**No**_____

Is supporting information available?   **Yes**_____**No**_____

What is it?_____Where is it?_____

Anecdotal Record Summary

Name: _____

Observer(s): _____

_____

This summary is based on_____records taken from

(no. of records)

_____ to _____

(date)   (date)

Is there supporting information on file?   **Yes**_____ **No**_____

If Yes, where is information located?_____

_____

Summary Statement:

Recommendations:

SIX

Another look — Observing instructional environments and teacher behavior

This chapter is designed to summarize information presented in the first five chapters. Thus, no new information will be presented. Unlike a conventional summary, however, this chapter will interpret concepts in a different perspective from which they were presented earlier. The perspective of this chapter is observation of the *instructional environment* of the learner. The basic principles and practices of observation are the same regardless of whether learners or instructional environments are being observed. So in this chapter we will take a look at the same information presented earlier, but we will consider the information as it applies to observing instructional environments and teacher behaviors rather than focusing directly on observing learner behaviors.

NECESSITY OF OBSERVING INSTRUCTIONAL ENVIRONMENTS

Throughout this book, the focus has been on observing learners for the purpose of making instructional decisions. We have portrayed the teacher as a "seeker of data." Observation has been defined as the process of systematically looking at and recording behavior for the purpose of making instructional decisions. For the most part, the "thing" that has been observed is the learner's behavior. Now that we are looking at observation methods from a slightly different perspective—that of the instructional environment—we need to modify the definition slightly and think of observing the operationally defined components of the instructional environment as the "thing" that is to be observed. We hasten to point out, however, that the major focus is still on the learner. We are observing the *components* of the instructional environment which is, of course, something different from learners' behaviors, but we are making these observations for the purpose of making instructional decisions for and about learners. It is usually the case that when information about the components of the instructional environment is added to information obtained about learner behavior, the resulting data base is stronger and allows us to make more justifiable inferences than if we were to base a decision only on the data about learner behavior.

Nothing New

Actually, although we didn't point it out at the time, we have illustrated the use of observational instruments to assess components of the instructional environments in previous chapters of the book. You may recall that in Chapter One we included a section on teacher behavior and discussed the idea that behaviors of learners and behaviors of teachers are very closely interrelated. We pointed out that it is important for teachers to monitor their own behaviors and to look closely at the relationship between their behaviors and the behaviors of learners. An example of a teacher was given in which the teacher was able to eventually determine that he was inadvertently reinforcing a child's "bothering" behaviors by paying attention to those behaviors whenever a child displayed them.

In Chapter Four, we presented an example of a checklist which an observer could use to record the availability of materials in the classroom and to assess the degree of access children had to those materials. This is another example of observing to determine an aspect of the instructional environment. Also in that chapter, we provided an activity which allows you to practice your skills in rating teacher behaviors.

We have not, then, neglected the observation of instructional environments totally, but we have certainly not focused heavily on it in earlier sections of the book. In this chapter we will look at components of instructional environments, how observation methods are used to observe these components, and the implications for instructional decision making arising from data collected by observing instructional environments.

We based our rationale for observing learner behavior on the principle that inferences about the characteristics of learners must be based on evidence which must be observable, and, in a similar vein, we feel that we can only make inferences about instructional environments when we have data about the components of those instructional environments.

COMPONENTS OF INSTRUCTIONAL ENVIRONMENTS

So, you want to observe instructional environments? *What* will you look at? What constitutes an instructional environment? We need to determine the variables present in instructional environments which have implications for the behavior of the learners. A global way to think of environment is that it is everything that surrounds us. The instructional environment would be everything that surrounds the learner.

We will consider four groups of variables which are present in instructional environments. It should be noted that in actual practice there is constant interaction among these variables. Although we have grouped them separately and will discuss them separately, in actual practice these items cannot be separated. We will consider the *other people* in the environment, the *space and objects* in it, the *time arrangements,* and the *management and teaching procedures* used within the environment.

People in the Instructional Environment

The other people present in the environment are part of the instructional environment. The teacher is the obvious person to be a part of the instructional environment. We must also consider the other learners as part of this environment. The ways in which other learners behave and the way in which learners and other adults interact set up an overall general climate or "feeling" within the classroom. This classroom climate influences each learner in different ways. Oftentimes there are other people in the classroom. Perhaps older children are involved in working with younger children. Perhaps one or several aides are working in the classroom. Perhaps there are parents, supervisors, or visitors present.

When thinking about the people in the instructional environment, we need to consider who they are, and we also need to think about how many of them there are. In open classroom situations, team teaching, continuous progress and non-graded situations, there may be large numbers of children functioning in the same space and in association with a large number of adults. These situations will influence learners in ways which are different from a smaller self-contained class-room situation in which fewer people are functioning.

Teacher Behaviors

Teacher behaviors are crucial components of the instructional environment. The ways in which teachers behave have important implications for the learning that occurs, or does not occur, in a classroom. Very often there is a discrepancy between what teachers think they are doing and what they are actually doing, and this discrepancy can often be discovered by teachers themselves, or pointed out to them, through the use of observation methods. When teachers have an opportunity to study records of their behavior, they often identify the discrepancy between what they view as desirable and intended teacher behavior and their actual behavior without too much difficulty or direct instruction. Perhaps some of you have had this experience already. Most teachers are surprised, some are even shocked, when they have an opportunity to review an observation record of their behavior. Just as learners need feedback to improve their performance, teachers need feedback to improve their teaching.

Space Variables

We need to consider space as part of the instructional environment. It is important to know how much space is available, what objects are included in that space, and

how those things are arranged. Ideally, different spaces will be available for different kinds of programs and activities. We expect learners to function differently in large, open spaces than they do in smaller, self-contained spaces. In fact, sometimes space arrangements will need to be modified so they match the characteristics of learners in order to promote their learning.

Another dimension of the instructional environment which is closely related to the space is that of instructional materials. In addition to an assessment of which materials are available, we are also interested in knowing how the materials are arranged and how accessible the materials are to the learners.

Time Variables

Time is another important dimension of the instructional environment. This aspect of the environment is not quite as tangible and obvious as instructional materials, but still it constitutes a part of the learning environment. The time variable involves considerations such as how routines are set up, what schedules are used in the classroom, whether children function in a variety of activities for large periods of time, or whether activities are of relatively short duration and are changed frequently. The numerous possibilities with regard to variation and the use of time, of course, have implications for the learning that occurs in the environment. Again, different time arrangements will be needed that are better suited to the particular characteristics of different learners.

Teaching Procedures and Management Practices

The instructional methods and management procedures which are carried out in a classroom also constitute a part of the instructional environment. These are variables which are sometimes fairly difficult to operationalize and observe, but they are a part of the learning environment and should be considered when observing.

Classroom environments are deliberately organized in different ways. In some types of programs, we expect certain behaviors to occur while we would hold very different expectations for the behaviors that occur in other types of programs. Consider the case of the traditional versus the open classroom. In the open classroom situation, by definition, many behaviors of the exploratory, inquiring, independent study type are expected, while more conventional types of behaviors are usually expected in more traditional classrooms. In reading, for example, we might expect children to write their own stories or to select their own books in an open situation, while we might expect them to read what is given to them in the more traditional classroom program.

If we were to develop checklists in the area of reading for each of these different classroom environments, the checklists would need to include very different items as derived from the different philosophies of the instructional program. A partial listing of items for checklists to be used in these situations follows:

Open Classroom
Reading Environment

1. A variety of trade books are shelved so that children can easily reach them.
2. Several rocking chairs, floor pillows, and a rug define the reading area.
3. A learning center on a topic such as "Long and Short Vowel Sounds" is set up.

Traditional Classroom
Reading Environment

1. A few trade books are in a display case outside the classroom entrance.
2. The reading circle is ten chairs, arranged in a semi-circle.
3. The basal readers are shelved near the reading circle.

These listings have been stretched a bit to illustrate differences in environments. Many traditional classrooms have an abundance of trade books, for example, even though our listings suggest this is not so.

INSTRUCTIONAL ENVIRONMENTS AND INSTRUCTIONAL DECISIONS

The instructional decisions typically made by teachers were presented in Chapter One. How can information about the components of the instructional environment enhance instructional decision making?

Deciding on Procedures and Materials

One of the major reasons teachers are interested in identifying relevant characteristics of learners is so that appropriate learning procedures and activities can be devised and instructional materials can be selected. Because of this, information about learners' reactions to certain teaching methods and materials could be gathered using observation methods. Suppose that a teacher is working with an intermediate level group of children in spelling. This teacher is interested in trying a programmed instruction procedure and a set of materials for teaching spelling. These particular materials are designed so that children work independently at their own rate. After introducing the new materials and the approach, the teacher assesses the children's reactions to the materials. A checklist of expected reactions and related considerations is prepared and, in addition, the teacher decides to keep careful anecdotal records of all the unanticipated reactions which are displayed. As a result of the information collected and interpreted regarding the reactions to the spelling materials, the teacher makes the decision to continue using the materials with part of the group and to introduce a different approach for use with another part of the group.

This is an example of an attempt to match instructional materials with children on the basis of information gathered through observing. It is also an example of arranging different instructional environments to suit the characteristics of the different learners since the environment which includes the programmed instructional materials is quite different from the environment in which another approach to teaching spelling is used.

Deciding on Objectives

Another of the instructional decisions made by teachers involves determining what to teach. Let's consider how this instructional decision is related to observation of the instructional environment. As a teacher observes a certain group of learners, he may determine that they are deficient in areas which might be generally described as "taking initiative or responsibility" for their own learning and "functioning independently" in learning. The teacher might decide that it is appropriate for children to engage in these behaviors and, therefore, might set up a series of instructional objectives intended to help children achieve these behaviors.

It is important to note that children cannot be expected to exhibit behaviors indicative of taking initiative and responsibility if the instructional environment precludes the display of these behaviors. For example, in a situation which is strongly teacher dominated and in which children are expected to pursue learning activities according to tightly regimented schedules, children simply do not have any opportunities to exercise their own initiative and take responsibility for their own learning. In deciding on the instructional objectives, then, the teacher must also decide simultaneously to arrange the instructional environment so that children have opportunities to display behaviors as specified in the objectives. Once the instructional environment is altered and some teaching procedures are instituted to enable children to reach the objectives, it is important for the teacher to observe the learner's achievement of objectives. It is also important for the teacher to observe the characteristics of the instructional environment in order to determine whether or not the environment allowed the expected behaviors to be exhibited.

Making Management Decisions

Another of the instructional decisions that teachers make concerns their management of behavior within the classroom. Many people refer to this as making decisions about how to discipline. One of the conclusions frequently reached by teachers when they observe their own disciplinary behaviors is that they are very often inadvertently teaching children to behave inappropriately. One of the most fruitful approaches for improving the teacher's behavior in this area is for the teacher to become adept at monitoring his own behavior in order to determine whether he is employing the techniques he intended to use.

For example, a teacher might be intending to focus on positive behaviors of children and to ignore, wherever possible, children's inappropriate behaviors with the idea that these inappropriate behaviors will then tend to drop out of the learner's behavioral repertoire. Upon observing his own behavior, the teacher may determine that he is paying attention to inappropriate behaviors even though he intended to ignore them. It should be obvious that this would be a possible explanation for the fact that the children may not have made any progress in eliminating the inappropriate behaviors. A fairly detailed example of this type of situation was presented in Chapter One, for a teacher who was, without realizing it, reinforcing a child's "bothering" behaviors.

Deciding to Seek Help

Another of the instructional decisions to be made by teachers concerns whether they need to enlist the aid of resource persons. If they decide they *do* need help from resource persons, then they must decide whom to ask for help. We already mentioned that we consider other people in the classroom as a component of the instructional environment. If teachers are going to enlist cooperation from other people, it is incumbent upon them to evaluate the effectiveness of this help. Observation procedures should be used to determine the changes in the instructional environment as they relate to the behaviors of the learner as a result of employing resource people within the classroom.

METHODS OF OBSERVING
AND RECORD KEEPING

We mentioned earlier that the gathering of information needed to make an instructional decision is the purpose for observation. The first step in the process of observation is to determine the purpose. Given that the purpose has been clearly stated, the observation process involves determining where to observe, when to observe, what to observe, who will do the observing, and how the observation will be recorded. Just as these five decisions in the observation process were used for assessing learner behaviors, they also apply to the assessment of operationally defined components within the instructional environment.

After the purpose for making the observation is determined, the type of record form to be used should be determined and the form should be developed for use. Then the actual observation or series of observations should be conducted and, finally, the interpretations needed to achieve the purposes for the observation should be made.

Tallying and Charting

Let's suppose that we have set up a series of learning centers within the classroom and are interested in determining which activities are used most frequently by children. For this purpose, a behavior tallying procedure would be most appropriate. In this case, of course, we would not tally behaviors, but rather we would tally instances of use of particular materials by learners. For a very gross index, we might simply list the names of the various learning centers and tally the number of children who go to each center during a given time period. Time-sampling procedures might be appropriate depending on the total organization of the school day and whether children have access to the learning centers all of the time or for only a limited period of time during the day. The information gathered through the behavior tallying procedures could then be charted in order to compare the demonstrated interests for the learning centers.

Suppose there were three learning centers in science, and a teacher was interested in determining which of the three was of most interest to the children. One of the centers was related to concepts about sound; another, concepts about electricity; and the third was based on the topic of simple machines. A behavior tallying procedure to be used for assessing children's interest in the three learning centers and the resulting tally chart and graph are shown on page 166. Note that "interest" is being operationally defined as the number of children who come to the center and work there for at least a 5-minute period of time. A new record form would be used each week if more information was needed.

Checklists, Rating Scales and Anecdotal Records

Checklists provide an efficient means of recording the presence or absence of specific behaviors in given situations. Now that we are focusing our attention on components of the instructional environment, we can think of checklists as also

Learning Center Interest Assessment

Week of: _____5/14/73_____

Observer: _____K. Wise_____

Directions: Each time a child comes to the center and spends at least five minutes there, enter a tally mark in the appropriate space.

Learning Center	Day					Total
	Mon.	Tues.	Wed.	Thurs.	Fri.	
Sound	〼 〼 〼 I	〼 〼 〼 IIII	〼 〼 〼 〼 II	〼 〼 〼 〼 III	〼 〼 〼 〼 II	107
Electricity	III	I	II	III	IIII	12
Simple Machines	〼 III	〼 II	〼	〼 II	〼 IIII	36

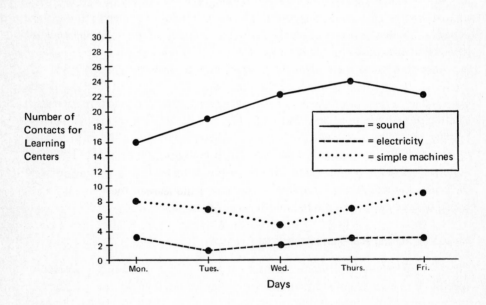

Observing instructional environments and teacher behavior

providing an efficient means of recording the presence or absence of certain components in given instructional environments. Also, whenever it is important to assess quality for dimensions of the environment, checklist-type items can be modified, quality scales developed, and the resulting rating scale can be used.

Suppose we are interested in certain model programs operating within a classroom and suppose it is essential that certain materials and procedures be occurring within a classroom in order to consider that classroom an instance of the model. A checklist might be developed to assess these components and, if the results of the checklist indicated that the classroom included a certain percentage of the components, it might then be labeled a "model classroom."

You will remember that one of the advantages of using a checklist is that a great deal of behavioral information can be recorded very rapidly. If we are interested in assessing teachers' verbal behaviors and if we can anticipate in advance the types of verbal statements we are looking for in teachers, we can develop these statements into a checklist and can then become much more efficient in our observation than if we had to laboriously copy verbatim dialogue of teachers in anecdotal record fashion.

Anecdotal records are probably the type of observation record that will be least useful in observing components of instructional environments. Generally the components will be things that can be anticipated in advance, and for this reason, anecdotal records will not be used frequently. This is not to say, of course, that anecdotal records will never be used because certainly there will be unanticipated occurrences within the classroom which will be worthy of record and in these instances anecdotal records will be the appropriate record-keeping device. Most of the unanticipated behaviors will probably revolve around teacher behaviors rather than variables of space, time, instructional materials, and procedures.

SUMMARY

This book has been devoted to the topic of using observations to help teachers make instructional decisions. The various chapters, taken in concert, should be helpful to the teacher in analyzing the behavior of the learner, the components of the instructional environment and the behavior of the teacher.

Chapter One addressed the question: Why use observation? It included a discussion of the instructional decisions that teachers make and some suggestions of other people who might want to observe and what their purposes might be. Chapters Two through Five were the "how to" chapters. Chapter Two presented the general principles involved in observing, and the other chapters focused on specific types of record keeping to be used with observations. Chapter Three presented information about behavior tallying and charting procedures. Chapter Four included information on the development and use of checklists, participation charts, and rating scales; Chapter Five was about using anecdotal records.

Finally, Chapter Six summarized the first five chapters and reinterpreted the information presented in those chapters from the perspective of the teacher and the instructional environment instead of the learner.